ON THE TOP OF
MOUNT PISGAH

GEORGE HANSAN

Library of Congress Control Number: 2019906902
ISBN: Softcover   978-1-7960-3662-6
          Hardcover   978-1-7960-3663-3
          EBook   978-1-7960-3661-9

Print information available on the last page

Rev. date: 06/06/2019

To order additional copies of this book, contact:
Xlibris
1-888-795-4274
www.Xlibris.com
Orders@Xlibris.com

Contents

1. Prologue. vii
2. Introduction ix
3. Wisdom to survive. 1
4. Born under the Japanese reign. 4
5. The Lee Family Tree. 5
6. My Childhood 7
7. Kindergarten and Seodang. 9
8. Young-Yi was lost. 10
9. A country bumpkin 11
10. Korea divided 13
11. Name of Jesus 16
12. Northern Korea 18
13. Exodus. 20
14. The Southern Korea. 22
15. Tae Pyoung Primary School. 23
16. "The Atomic Bomb of Love". 24
17. Joyful Sunday-School. 25
18. Korean War. 26
19. Uncle Jae Kook 28
20. Refugee Life. 30
21. Memorable Sunday school in refuge life. . . . 32
22. Junior High Period. 33
23. The first fight. 34
24. A student's testimony 35
25. Armistice Agreement 36
26. Mother was great 38
27. 시 Poem. 39
28. A Proof of Being Chosen. 41
29. High School Period 42
30. Flexibility of a rule. 44
31. Act as a midwife 45
32. 4. 19. Revolution 46
33. Korea awakened 47
34. Turbulent times 48
35. Attending Christian school 49
36. Turning point 50
37. Broad-minded people. 52
38. One-day honeymoon. 53
39. A hybrid at home 54
40. 시 Poem. 55
41. Dad, what made you come to America?* . . . 56
42. "This is the right country." 57
43. 시 Poem. 60
44. Do you have a job opening? 61
45. Meeting Mr. Tochstad. 62
46. American dream 63
47. Epilogue. 65

ON THE TOP OF
MOUNT PISGAH

(Deuteronomy 34:1)

PROLOGUE

My dear children,

I arrived at Honolulu airport on September 20, 1968(confirmed by the old Korean passport).

I entered the United States of America as a graduate student to study Business Administration (MBA) at Oregon State University at Corvallis, Oregon. Two years later your mom, Susan and James came to this country. Helen was born in Los Angeles in 1972.

I once had a keen regret that I had brought you to the United States of America. All kinds of crimes by guns, juvenile delinquency, drug and child abuse that I had never heard of when I was in Korea made it regretful – ironically all kinds of crime were few in absolute poverty in Korea while it has a lot of crime nowadays in material abundance (within the 10th place economically world-widely).

At the Kimpo airport before departure per NWA, At that time Korea did not have any Int'l Airlines

It made me think of a passage of the novel, "Tess of the D'Urbervilles" written by Thomas Hardy;

"The Egypt of one family was the land of Promise to the family who saw it from a distance, till by residence there it became it turns their Egypt also."

Yes, America looked like The Land of Promise when I saw it from a distance but it was also another Egypt. However, this is yet the land to come to because I found out this is *the land of the free and the home of the brave* as the National anthem (The star spangled banner) says.

They often say "American dream". Though this may have lost its luster, the United States is known as the land of freedom and opportunity. That, too, could be applied to me. Commonly I hear they use this term when someone is remarkably successful in business or wins a great fame. Truly I say to you; do not think American dream is in success in business or in fame only.

Please remind yourselves of the spirit and the faith of The Pilgrims Fathers.

I wish I could enter Canaan with you, but it is a pity that I cannot help staying at the east of the Jordan because of many reasons. Nevertheless, I exalt the name of the Lord which guided me to the top of Mount Pisgah to show the Promise (opportunity) land to my children where they will live with a dream and walk in the faith in God.

Children, Have great dreams. Conquer Canaan with your faith.

To conquer this land means to contribute to this country.

Canaan was not *"a good and spacious land, a land flowing with milk and honey"*. It was a barren, sterile and infertile land. Many enemies to fight against were there.

Why did the Lord say to Moses that it was *"a land flowing with milk and honey"*? I interpret it has the spiritual meaning; you will possess milk and honey spiritually since you enter the promise land. I would like to leave the question for you to consider the meaning why God said to Moses *"a good and spacious land, a land flowing with milk and honey"*.

There might be a big Jericho in front of you or you could meet a little Ai. Whatever you may meet you must ask for God's will beforehand. Do not go ahead without asking him.

America in my prayer cannot become Egypt.

"Trust in the Lord with all your heart and lean not on your own understanding. Acknowledge him in all your ways and he will make your path straight." (Proverbs 3:5-6)

Michael and Susan, James and Donna, Dean and Helen, You are the Joshua and the Caleb for the Valenzuela, the Lee and the Syn. I want to give you some words which were given to the young by Joshua before his death. These words also had been given to Joshua by the Lord after Moses' death before crossing the Jordan;

Joshua 23:6 *"Be very strong; be careful to obey all that is written in the Book of the Law of Moses, without turning aside to the right or to the left. 7Do not associate with these nations that remain among you; do not invoke the name of their gods or swear by them. 8But you are to hold fast to the Lord your God, as you have until now."*

9 "The Lord has given out before you great and powerful nations; to this day no one has been able to withstand you. 10 One of you routs a thousand, because the Lord your God fights for you, just as he promised. 11 So be very careful to love the Lord your God."

---Joshua 23:6-11---

I began writing this story to comply with Susan's request.

One day she said, *"My children won't know about our family root someday at all, Dad…"*

She added, *"What shall I say to our children about our family root when they grow up enough?"*

I thank Susan for having given such a meaningful suggestion to me.

Certainly, the family root is important for my descendants to be able to identify themselves. Moreover, I would like to say that the real purpose of this writing about my insignificant life is to let my children know how faithful and great the Lord's grace has been throughout my life. He has chosen our family among 20,000,000 people in northern Korea. He had made us leave the hell of North Korea before the cruel communist tyranny began. I believe He provided a way for our family to avoid the dreadful suffering and misery. The Lord moved us to Seoul, Korea in 1946 and He moved me again to the free land of America at His time.

I hope you can see how He has been guiding me, how He fed me and how He protected me as my shepherd during the Japanese control, during the Korean War and during the Korean political and social chaos or disorder. I hope this poor writing can give some help for my posterity to know how great God's love is.

On the one hand I am glad I can write my story in English for my posterity to be able to read it, but on the other hand frankly speaking I do not know how much my story will attract my children's attention because my English writing ability has its origin not in a real life from youth in America but in the school English text book as a second language. I tried not to make any mistake in grammar.

INTRODUCTION

Before starting my own account,

I would like to introduce a classmate Hong, Chung-IL, of my high school days. I was a model student while he was unusual in his behavior and attitude.

He was one of the strongest guys in fight in the classes.

He was neither a rowdy boy nor a hooligan though.

He was just a good fighter. He was a son of a pastor.

The reason why I am introducing this friend to you is for you not to see a people in prejudice or partiality and you should know some peoples' thought or thinking way is entirely incredibly different from your thought or your way of thinking.

I just want you not to make any mistakes among the people with a biased view.

However, I want to make one thing clear.

I am not saying he was a successful man. I reckon the real success is to fulfill the dream in accord with God's providence.

Susan   Helen   Jame

Hong, Chung IL's brief personal history:

A Seoul City Councilman (**구위원**)

A Director of Saemaul Financial Firm

The owner of a western-style clothes shop (boutique)

A druggist (fake) of a pharmacy during the disorder period after the war.

WISDOM TO SURVIVE

"I want to sleep at your house tonight, Young-George."

Chung-IL said to me who was a classmate of Dae Kwang(great light) High School.

He would pay a visit to me and sleep in my room from time to time, especially during the period of mid-term test or final test.

He also asked me the same favor that night as he used to ask of;

"Young- George, please pick out five exam questions of Math in expectation for tomorrow's test and explain them to me."

I did it to him as he asked.

He always seemed he could hardly understand my explanations.

However, he memorized them completely in writing without whole understanding the problems and the answers and immediately he went to bed while I continued studying for tomorrow's exam.

"How did the test go?" I asked him.

"It was Okay." He answered smiling.

His average mark was not bad at all among his peer who mingled with him in physical strength. As a matter of fact his school academic record was the top among them.

"You know what…, Young- George."

"As I am given an examination paper I write down my name neatly and I start to compare questions of the test paper with the questions in my memory. If I find the same questions given by you I write down the answers as you gave to me.

The other questions that I do not know I cross out them with a pencil and I write down the questions in my memory with the answers that were given by you. The following day, I visit the teacher who teaches the subject and I beg him to manage it all right saying, "Teacher, you know I am not eligible to go to college and I know myself so well that I know I cannot even graduate from this high school without your help. All that I know is that I must be a graduate from a high school to get a job. Please help me to graduate from this high school."

This was his confession. He added that he gave the teacher a big formal deep bow as soon as he entered the teacher's room. At any rate, he graduated from the high school.

It was toward the evening on a day before graduation he came to visit me at home. He wanted to spend the night with me.

I perceived intuitively he had some exquisite matter to say to me because all the examinations were over.

I precisely remember what he said to me at that night;

"Young- George, after graduation I want to live my life helping my friends like you. I do not have any intellectual faculties as you know, but I have the power of my fist. After graduation I will go out to the square of Seoul Railroad Station and I can take over the reins of the gangsters in that area in one month. I want to help my friends with the power of my fist."

His talk was astounding and beyond my thought.

At the moment I heard it I was speechless because it was no joke at all. The tone of his voice was calm and serious. I remember his talk was continued somehow and I was not listening to him any more though.

I remember I did not say anything back to him that night.

Next morning my mother prepared breakfast for us as she used to do it. Chung IL and I sat down at the table face to face. About the time when we finished the breakfast I told him my opinion about his intention to live helping friends by the power of his fist.

"I appreciate your thought to help me in the future.
I would rather ask you not to go out to the square of the Seoul Railroad Station. You could have some other ways to help me in some opportunities. I am afraid that no other friends want to be helped by the power of your fist either."

He did not go out to the square of Seoul Railroad Station after all. He was hired as a helper of a pharmacist in a pharmacy and he worked there for several years. One day he came to see me.

"Young George, I want to marry a girl. Would you have a good look at her how she is?"
I asked him in return, *"Why do you want to marry her?"*
He said, *"She is very obedient."*
"How obedient is she?"
"What did you ask her to do?" I asked to him.
His answer was also remarkable and beyond my thought.
He said, *"I told her to stay up on her knees by my side whole night while I sleep and she did it as I had told her."*

I met her with him and I asked her in front of him if she could cope with his radical personality. She said, *"Yes."* They got married. They opened a western-dressmaking shop (a boutique). His wife was a designer of Occidental clothes. She taught him about all sorts of texture and how to buy the materials in Dong Dae Moon (East Gate) market place.

He seemed to have learned quickly whole things in purchasing the materials. Their business was so successful that they could build a little building of three stories whose structure was formed three rooms on each floor. They used three rooms on the third floor as their residential quarters. Two shops on the ground floor as their stores and the other one was rented to another merchant. Three rooms on the second floor were rented to other people as living quarters.

About the building arrangement my memory could be inaccurate.

Since I came to the States I met him a few times when I visited Korea. I learned he had died in sixties. His career was as follows as I heard from other friends;

He became meek, faithful and humble.
H was hired as a clerk by Saemaul Financial Firm.
He became a director of Saemaul Financial Firm.
He was elected as Seoul City Councilman (구의원)

BORN UNDER THE JAPANESE REIGN

I was born on November 3, 1936 at 47 Kyo-Dong, Bukjin-Eub, Unsan-Kun, Pyeonganbuk-Do, Korea. My grandparents had four sons and one daughter; My father was the fourth child and the third son. My father's name was Won Byeok Lee and my mother's name was Jae Hak Lee (Ro). The family origin is Won Ju – Lee family. My mother's family origin is Kwang-Ju – Ro.

I was born under the Japanese control.
I was influenced by a Japanese from the birth.
My father worked in an engine room of the gold mine.
The supervisor was a Japanese.
I was told by my father that he was an honest and faithful man.
So was my father and they became good friends to speak each other without restraint. My father never mentioned his name at all though.

This is the story that my mother told me many years later after my father's decease;
I actually was born on November 2, 1936.
My father naturally told the Japanese friend (literally the supervisor of his workplace) about my birth. My father was known as a man of his word and honest telling no lie so that the supervisor liked him and trusted in him.
He was told I was born around eleven o'clock at night on November the 2nd. His response was quick and clear to say,

"One hour is not a big thing."
"Why don't you make it November 3?"
"November 3 is the birthday of MaiJi Dennoheiga"
(MaiJi The Heavenly Emperor – the founder of The Reformed Japan).

This is how my birthday has become November the third about.
My father seemed to follow his opinion since he meant good and my birthday was registered as November the third in 1936.

I left my birth-place when I was eight and I do not remember much about my father's brothers. I remember my aunt (gomo, father's elder sister) who had one daughter, my cousin, and another cousin called Young Baek whose father was the first son of my grandparents.

THE LEE FAMILY TREE

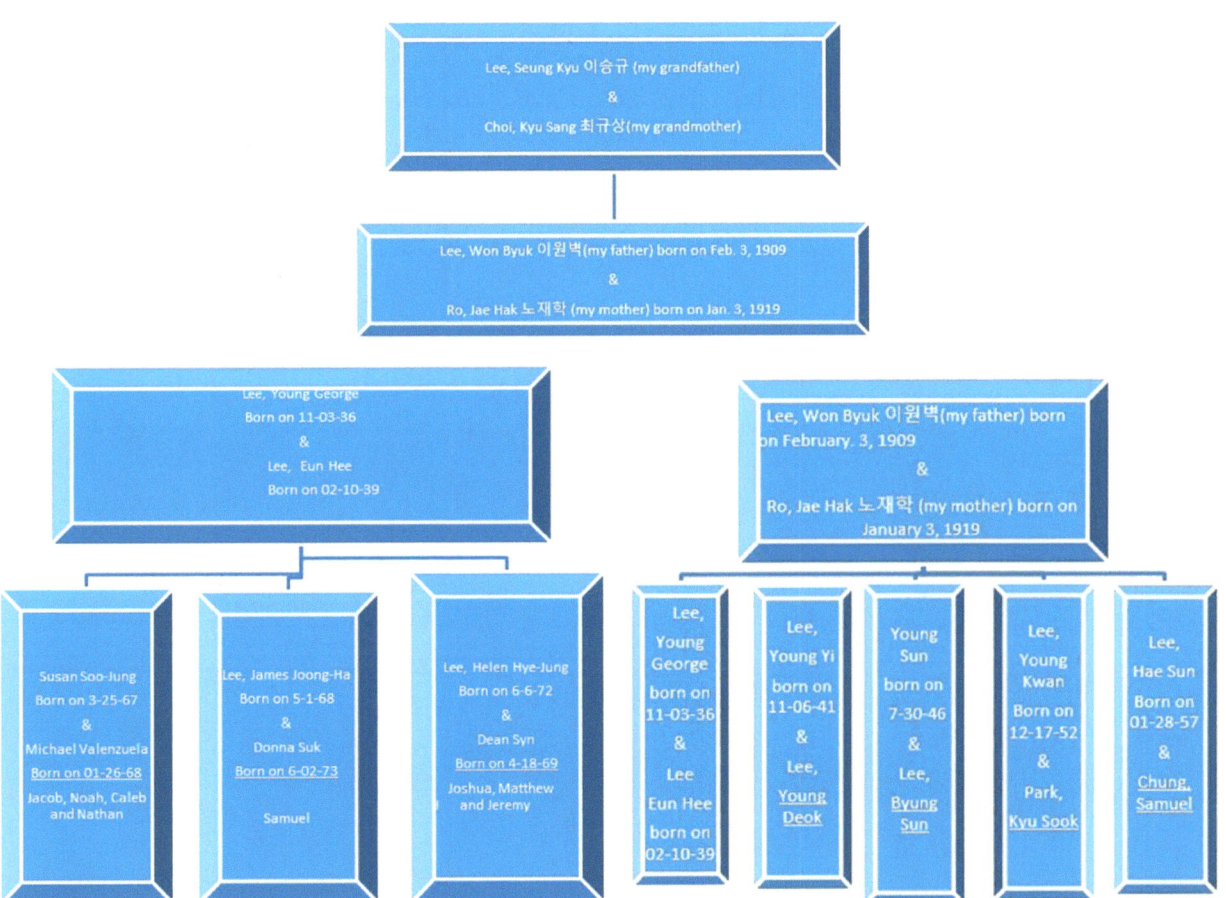

I was told that my grandparents had passed away when I was about one or two years old. I remember my aunt's feature and image. She was graceful and refined. She had a fair complexion.

I remember she would bring generous gifts to me whenever she called on our family. My father and mother would bow to her in civil and friendly manner whenever she paid us a visit.

I remember our house was neat. It was located in the central area of the town. Unsan was a little town developed early in the northern Korea due to the gold mining. The reserves and deposits of gold were so great in the surrounding mountains and its output of gold won it the first place nationwide. According to the changes of proprietorship of mining rights Chinese town was formed and American town and Japanese town in that sequence.

It was an international and beautiful town;

A creek meanders through it. A river was flowing along the outland. I do not remember the name of the river.

One thing that I clearly remember is that the river was the place where I was once drowned. I drowned myself down to the bottom of the river. From the bottom of the water I could see my friends swimming around above and I could hear someone's crying out, *"Where is Young George?"* and simultaneously a big guy dived in and pulled me out of the water. Probably at that time I was four or five years old. I was too young to remember the big guy's name even though I owed him my life. The town was influenced by the Western Civilization. I can recall good schools were there and the landscaping was westernized around the kindergarten which I recognized far later after I grew up.

I remember that the kindergarten which I attended had beautiful structures and was well landscaped. It was located by the American town in the forested place.

The playground was big and filled with straight upright larches maintaining proper distance between them.

I am afraid that most of children in those days did not ever know about the kindergarten education even for those children in the big cities in Korea. Fortunately I could finish the good kindergarten called Kwang Myung Yuchiwon which meant Bright Light Kindergarten.

MY CHILDHOOD

I was brought up hearing so many interesting stories from my grand-mother (wae-halmuni, my mother's mother).

She was living with her first son (my uncle, my woe-samchon) about five blocks away from our house. Her stories were about tigers, cats, magpie, crow, a huge serpent and foxes which were one thousand years old and they were able to be transfigured into a human being. No one told me about the bible stories until I became a ten year old boy.

I often think of the stories that I heard from my grandmother.

I would like to tell you one of them;

Once upon a time, there was a straw thatched cottage in a remote and secluded glen of deep mountains, where a mom, a papa, a son and a daughter were living. The cottage was tucked away deep in the woods. The brother and the younger sister were waiting for their parents from the farm work. It gets dark quickly there because the cottage was in the deep glen among the big and high mountains. Until late night their parents did not come home. They waited and waited. They were getting hungry and scared as the night grew darker and pitched. They locked the door tightly as their parents had told them beforehand.

Suddenly the sound of touching the door iron-ring handle to try to open the door.

"Who is it?"

They asked as they had been instructed by their father.

My grandmother would pause at the moment of such a thrilling story and then I felt a chill and thrilled with horror.

"Your mom." *was the response.*

"Your voice sounds not like our mom's voice."

"I am tired and that is why"

A dead silence was there for a minute.

"May I see your hand?"

The tiger could not disguise its hairy hand and it started growling and scratching the door.

The scratching and growling were getting harder and louder. The brother and the sister began to escape through the back door and ran and ran.

Finally the tiger crushed the door to enter the room.

As soon as the tiger found out they were not in, its running after them began. The brother and the sister ran and ran but they could not run so fast as the tiger. The tiger was getting closer and closer. The brother and the sister prayed to the mountain god to save them from the tiger. Suddenly a strong rope came down from the heaven in front of them. Both of them started to climb up the rope. The tiger could not climb up the rope after them. They climbed and climbed and reached the heaven. The sister was afraid of the night and became the sun in daytime and the brother became the moon bravely at night.

I still remember how terrified I was listening to the stories.

In the most of her stories no names of the characters were told.

I think this kind of folk tales imply some hidden meanings.

She was a great story teller to me. Her stories were endless; about one hundred year old fox, about cats and about a huge serpent and magpies. Also Korean classic novels; <u>Shimchungjeon,</u> <u>Janghwa Hongryun Jeon</u>, <u>Honggildong jeon</u>, <u>Imggeokjung jeon</u>, <u>Kongjui and Pahtjui</u> and etc.

Kindergarten and Seodang

As I recall this memory I feel yearning for my father.

It was about the time ending the autumn season and entering into the winter. My father brought a brand-new stylish overcoat with him to the kindergarten to take me home.

My father succinctly said, *"It suddenly became so cold that I bought this coat for you."* He brought also an air gun to catch sparrows to roast them for me in that evening.

My father sent me to "Seodang" after kindergarten instead of a regular elementary school because Japan occupied Korea and controlled the school education and we had to learn Japanese compulsorily instead of Korean. Speaking Korean in the school was forbidden.

"Seodang" was a village school-house. Seodang was a private home school teaching Chinese classics translating it into Korean.

I remember the number of the students in the class was less than seven in all. Reflecting my childhood of "Seodang" school-house I

find myself who was afraid of the teacher with a long rod, which was used to make students silent. Fortunately Japanese government could not control such a little private school. I presume my father might think it was better for me to learn Chinese characters than Japanese for my future. Actually the study at Seodang helped me later in many ways. Korean newspapers were printed in Korean characters but half mixed with Chinese characters. I could easily read and understand the papers while most friends of my age had inconvenience in reading them.

One thing I did not like was the location of the Seodang.

It was too far away from our house. I had to walk for a long time.

I do not remember how far it was but it was a tiresome distance.

I remember I did not go to school one day and just ate lunch (doshirak) on the way to school and wandered here and there and came home at the proper time. Afterwards, my father had to leave Unsan, his born-place. He took us – mom, me and my younger brother Young Yi – to a remote secluded country place in the mountains called Chosan, Young Byun, to avoid his being drafted into Japanese army work.

YOUNG-YI WAS LOST

Young Yi, my younger brother, was born on November 6, 1941.

I recall my brother Young Yi was lost on the way to Chosan, Young Byeon. Whenever I hear about an abduction or lost case of children I recall the misfortune of my brother's being lost.

I was frustrating, tantalizing and upsetting.

My mother expressed later about the feeling when we had lost him as follows: *"My heart was devastated and burned to charcoal."*

We lost him before lunch time and I found him at dusk at the starting point. He was standing in front of the inn where we had stayed one night and had left after breakfast. I ran and ran along the road that we had passed that morning looking all over the places and alleys. I was eight years old and Young Yi was only three.

Still I do not understand how he was lost and how he went back that far to the starting point and recognized the place and standing there. Yes, He was crying at the pace where we had left that morning. Only God's grace could explain it. What if I had not been to the starting point – the inn?

The number of the lost during the Korean War was innumerable but any single one of our family was not lost. It was not by our effort and not by our wisdom either. It was entirely by His grace.

A COUNTRY BUMPKIN

We stayed at Chosan, Young Byun, until we met the "Liberation Day" (free from Japanese control), - August 15, 1945.

There I attended a regular elementary school.

I remember I walked about five miles (?) along the mountain road every day to go to school and to return home. It was a long and scary way for a little boy. Sometimes I tucked up the crotches of my trousers and waded across the brook to school.

I am to mention the Japanese supervisor of my father's work place here again. This is the details of the reason why we moved to this remote and secluded place in the mountains; One day approaching the end of the World War II the supervisor called my father and said, *"Drafting even middle aged men into the army work (not fighter but work draft) will begin soon and so you quickly go to the remote country with your family and stay there for the time being."*

Our family owed him a lot humanely and my father missed him a lot. He was an angel for our family.

God has chosen us and loved us before we knew Him.

His hand was with us before we knew Him.

Before class, every morning, we had to stand up and give attention to a tiny temple-like wooden ware "Gamidana"- means god's altar, which was hanging above the blackboard to make a pledge of allegiance to the country – to Japan's Heavenly Emperor.

At that time the "Heavenly Emperor" of Japan was the god for Japanese people like the emperor Caesar of Rome.

I remember I was punished for hours standing straight in the middle of the playground on account of speaking Korean in the school because I violated the rule; *"You must not speak Korean."*

We were forced not to speak Korean in the school.

On that day I was given a detention to clean school toilets.

I was attending school without knowing our own country had been taken away by Japan because I was too young and I was told neither at home, at kindergarten nor Seodang because they might have thought children were too young to understand whole things.

Perhaps my father also did not tell me about it because of my age. I remember I heard that my father once said that there was no need to throw away my life for no purpose when we moved to this remote country. I did not know what it meant either.

We were impelled to write letters to the so-called Imperial Soldiers, which were called "Consolation Letters" at that time.

Ironically the letter that I wrote was chosen as the best Consolation Letter and I was awarded a little prize by the same teacher who gave me the detention of cleaning school toilets.

In a morning assembly on the school playground the principal said,

"I have a good news to announce to you students this morning. Our enemy's president Roosevelt died. We will give three cheers for his death in unison." "Banzai, Banzai, Banzai."

Banzai means Hurray.

He did not mention the name of the country in my memory.

I just remember "Our enemy's president".

In fact I did not recognize the president's name at that time because the name was too long and so strange to me that I had never heard.

Actually I did not know he was our enemy either.

In those days when the World War II was about to end we were forced to bring the brassware to the school and to go to the mountains to collect pine resin. The Japanese army was so desperate that they had to collect brassware and pine resin for the war supplies.

Of course I did not know who needed such things until I was told my father's explanation after the World War II.

They called them brass scraps but they were our families' indispensable necessaries. At that time most of our precious kitchen wares were made of brass, which were used for every meal and especially for the religious or memorial services according to Confucian ritual.

At that time one of my friends who was only 9 years old got married suddenly with a girl who was 14 years old.

We made fun of him and played jokes on him even though we did not know about marriage.

They said the sudden marriage was made for the bride to avoid drafting by Japanese Imperial Army. Before very long with my own eyes I saw a girl was being drafted to the Japanese Imperial Army. She was taken away being seen off on the Japanese army truck. At that time I was not aware that it was a draft of a Comfort Woman [girl]; Japanese military sex slaves. The issue of Comfort Woman has been proved by Japanese historians based on the records of Japanese Imperial Army, but Abe government of Japan has been trying to deny and twist the historical fact.

How pity it is!

The Japanese premier Abe is teaching how to tell a lie for the purpose to its people and its innocent children, while on the other side of the earth Angela Merkel, the Chancellor of Germany, apologized twice to the war victims admitting their criminal acts during the World War II.

Japan must apologize for having stamped down the rights of Korean young women during the World War II. This matter is not only for the rights of Korean women but also for the rights of whole women on the earth. The image of God was trampled by Japanese. This crime should be revealed widely to the world.

Therefore the comfort woman statue must be set up at the proper spots throughout the world.

I personally just feel shameful that our ancestors did not strengthen our national defense power by accepting western modern civilization spontaneously at the same time as Japan accepted the western modern civilization in Meiji Reforms.

Even nowadays the left wing political power of Korea is losing the eye to see the whole picture of the flow of the world.

The Comfort Woman Statue – Actually Sex Slave for Imperial Japanese Army

Korea divided

On August 15, 1945 The unconditional surrender of Imperial Japan was announced and formally signed on September 2, 1945.

The World War II ended by the American atomic bombings on Hiroshima and Nagasaki in Japan. Korea was liberated from the Japan's 35 years' occupation.

Shouts of joy and tears of Koreans were followed and the streets were filled with people dancing around.

We also had big celebration. A big gathering was in our school.

I remember my teacher made me sing a song on the platform which was set up temporarily in the school playground.

At that time we were living at Chosan, Young Byun in Pyeongahn-Buk-Do. I mentioned earlier this remote country place was the district of my father's shelter to avoid Japanese military forced labor draft.

About a month before the end of the World War II in my memory

I had experienced a strange thing.

One of my father's uncles was staying with us.

I was told to call him "Harabuji". I never asked my parents why they had come to our house and how long they would be going to stay with us. His grandson's name was Chang Geun.

On that day I was with the "Harabuji" in the

The Comfort Woman Statue – Actually Sex Slave for Imperial Japanese Army

same room. All of sudden a big shake (earthquake) with a roar was felt and some stuffs fell down from the shelves. He said, *"Chinese or Russian might be coming down this time. When Japanese came into our country before, the quake had come from the east."*

I would rather say he was mumbling by himself.

I do not remember how many days passed. I heard Russian soldiers had come into Korea.

Tragedy to Korean people!

Southern Korea was liberated from Japanese control by American forces and northern Korea by Russian forces according to the Yalta Conference held in April, 1945 at Yalta in the Crimea.

Pathetically Korea was divided into two by the 38th parallel - 38 degrees north latitude; north-communist country and south-democratic country.

However, I came to know lately it was rather fortunate for Korea because the Communist could entirely take over whole Korea;

The U.S. army forces was far away from Korea at the time of war ending while the Russian army forces was almost entering Korean peninsula. **The U.S. government** urged the negotiating line should be as much farther toward north as possible while **the U.S. army** insisted on that the war ending line should be between Korea and Japan because there were not enough army forces to dispatch far up to Korea.

Without this esteemed person 50,000,000 Korean people could live under the reign of Kim's inhumane despotism - Kim IL Sung, Kim Jung IL and Kim Jung Eun.

The esteemed person was not a Korean but an American.

In Korean history it was the first time that a nation's fate was decided by a single foreigner.

As we think of the ending of the World War II General Douglas McArthur comes across Koreans' mind.

The president of the United States of America, Harry S. Truman was forgotten as the benefactor.

Not a few people have a view that Korea could have been communized early in 1960 like Vietnam if we had not have Korean War in 1950.

The greatest reason why Korean War broke up on June 25, 1950 was due to the withdrawal of the U.S Armed Forces from Korea The U.S. military authorities made decision that they could not defend Korea and did have no need to defend it. That was why they withdrew the U.S. Armed Forces from Korea one year before the Korean War.

Why did America save Korea from the communists?

54,246 American soldiers died and 100,000 soldiers were wounded in Korean War.

Both countries did not have any mutual alliance agreement at that time.

Who dispatched 150 thousand military forces to Korean War?

It was the president Harry S. Truman.

The secretary of State of America, Dean Acheson, reported to the president Harry Truman on June 24, 1950 as follows: *"Sir, it is very serious news. North Korean Army generally invaded South Korea. According to the report from the ambassador Muccio in Korea it is a quite different invasion from the previous attacks.*

I requested the U.N. Security Council to the Secretary-General of the United Nations." The president was spending the week-end at his home town in the state of Missouri.

According to one report the president Truman said, *"We must stop sons of bitch by all means."* It became known that it took 10 seconds for him to make such a decision.

He pondered long and deeply over it flying back to Washington A.B by the presidential plane Independence;

< It came to his mind that the invaders had continued such bad conducts because the democratic countries had neglected and had not stopped such attacks.

If the communists' bad conducts are not stopped by the free world and are allowed to attack Korea without any deterrence the little countries around the strong communist countries cannot endure their threats and their offensive.

If this invasion is neglected the World War III could occur as the similar incidents brought the World War II.>

Truman said, *"I swear by God that I will make them pay the cost for this attack."* in the limousine to the Blair House.

This thankful story about the president Harry Truman is somewhat diminished according to "The Coldest Winter" published in 2015 by Hyperion, the writing of David Halberstam, a New York Times Bestseller.

Children, here I want to interpose a part of my prayer.

This prayer of mine was written for the service at Young Nak Presbyterian church in Los Angeles in August 1998.

"Father God, Thank you for your blessings upon our mother country Korea. Korea has 5000 years of history but it had been extremely poor. Our people had to live in destitution as poor as a church mouse. Our country could not decide our own fate with our own will. The destiny of our country has been decided by Beijing, Tokyo, Moscow, Washington and London.

Nevertheless, Father God, you blessed our little country so much that one century ago you sent us a few faithful servants such as Underwood, Allen and Appenzeller from America to give your light to our people in darkness. Now it has become the 2nd *country after America in number of dispatching missionaries world widely. Lord, we pray for your continuous blessings upon Korea so that your name may be glorified throughout the world. They will say," God chose the foolish things of the world to put to shame the wise; God chose the weak things of the world to put to shame the strong." Corinthians 1:27* The rest is omitted.

Korea is a peninsula. The northern side is connected with China and Russia and the other three sides are surrounded by the seas; West side faces *Whang Hae*, East side *Dong Hae(Japanese Sea)* and South side *Nam Hae*. Korea was surrounded by the strong countries; China, Japan and Russia and historically it was used like a bridge when China made inroads into Japan and Japan made its way into China. Korea was invaded by neighboring countries innumerably. Nevertheless, Koreans defeated them and kept the state.

They underwent many difficulties, afflictions and calamities but they have not lost their identity as Korean people.

Korea has the history of 5000 years.

Unfortunately Korean history was distorted widely by Japanese.

I think it has been authentic considerably by Korean historians.

My dear children, I hope you will have an opportunity to read about Korean history. They have not lost their own language and they have kept their letters (Hangeul), which was created by King SeJong the Great of Yi Dynasty, which played the important role to keep Korean identity.

I believe Korean character (HanGeul) is the evidence of God's blessing upon Korea. The theory of *the survival of the fittest* **cannot explain about the survival of Korea among the Great Powers.**

It can be explained "only by God's Grace and Providence."

I would say it was a miracle.

The Hangeul (Korean alphabet) is the best letters in the world, which has been recognized and proved in the linguistic society.

NAME OF JESUS

It was a scenario of God's grace toward our family;

In 1945 a few months before the end of World War Two Cholera rubbished our family. I got it first. Cholera's symptom was mild with me. About five days later I got recovered.

The cholera's symptom of my father was severe with high fever and watery vomiting accompanied by diarrhea.

My mother tailed after my father's sickness. My father and my mother said idle words and silly talks. Both of them saw phantom or illusion. Our home was devastated.

My grandmother (wae-halmoni) who lived in Jin Nam Po, a west coast harbor city urgently came and took care of them until they were all recovered. I would still recall I had been cooking rice as a nine year old boy until my wae-halmoni came. Wae-Halmoni urged us to move out of Chosan Youngbyun to Jin Nam Po.

We moved from Chosan Youngbyun, Pyeonganbuk-Do to Jin Nam Po, a harbor city approximately 15 miles away to the west from Pyeong Yang of Pyeongannam-Do, in the northern Korea.

My uncle's (woe-samchon, my mother's brother) family was living there at Uknanggi in the city. I attended Bong Dae elementary school for one semester there. Jin Nam Po is a very memorable place for me because it was the place where I was led to the Sunday school by my youngest aunt, Jae Hyun imo (mother's youngest sister) who was working for the post office and learned about Jesus Christ. It was the first time for me to have heard about Jesus and the bible. I sang hymns. The hymns I learned for the first time were "What a Fellowship, What a Joy Divine" and "This is My Father's World". When I sang the hymns I felt that they were entirely different songs from those that I had sung before in the school. Yes, I felt something different that I could not express.

The worship was an unprecedented experience.

I was just happy to go to Sunday school. I became a boy waiting for Sunday from Monday. Aunt Jae Hyun (imo) used to wake up early in the morning to go to church six days a week for the dawn prayer meeting. Unfortunately she remained in the northern Korea.

Throughout my life whenever I go to church for the dawn prayer meeting I yet think of Jae Hyun imo and pray for her and the people in North Korea.

Could I expect that she is still alive?

I do believe she has never lost her faith in Jesus in any situation.

How hard and miserable her life should have been through under the tyranny of the communist dictator's regime if she is alive!

Why and how is God just watching the groaning of the people under the communist ruthless tyranny of the dictator?

What is the Lord's will? Lord, I believe you are watching over the Christians in North Korea.

On July 30, 1945 Young-Sun was born.

Late Summer in 1946 we came down to the southern Korea but aunt Jae Hyun Imo was left in the northern Korea; This is how my Imo could not come down to the southern Korea with us;

Imo was living with us after my wae-halmuni had gone down to the southern Korea to be with her son's family. We loved her so much that my heart is tingling as I think of her.

There was a young man at our next door when we were living in Jeong Joo, Pyunganbuk-Do. My grandmother (wae-halmuni) wanted Imo to marry him but she did not like him. The young man came down to the south with my grandmother.

In the nick of time Imo happened to meet a young man whose parents were living at our neighbor village and he was attending Kim Il Sung University in Pyeong Yang. His feature was elegant and handsome. Imo met him a few times and became to like him. Her marriage was naturally hastened because it had to be done before our departure to the southern Korea.

Northern Korea

Russian soldiers trampled the northern Korea with their submachine guns. They called themselves "Liberation Army". They rode a horse carrying a loaf of bread without any wrap under their armpit. They carried many wristwatches on their arms as spoils. I still remember *"Dawaii"* which means "Give it to me" in Russian.

I was told that as soon as Russian soldiers see watches on Koreans' wrists they right away said, *"Dawaii"* and took them away. Many wrist watches on their forearms proved the rumor was true.

One night my father said, *"We will move to the south."*

Next morning we were about to go out to the street but the streets to the harbor were blocked with CLOSED signs which were set up during the night.

The ostensible reason was because of the epidemic of cholera.

We heard many people had been moving to the south by vessels secretly and my father's plan was also to escape by a vessel through the Jin Nam Po harbor. Incidentally my mother decided to move to Jeong Joo, Pyeonganbuk-Do, my mother's born-place;

where many people who had the family name "Ro" formed a big village. My mother's uncles, aunts, cousins, second cousins and relatives welcomed our family with delight. Now I can imagine and meditate how Noami's return to her relatives was. Naomi's return was pathetic, but my mom's return was delightful.

I attended O-Chun(means five creeks) elementary school for one semester there.

The activity of members of Communist Party was zealous.

They called meetings almost every evening to make propaganda for Communism.

Their slogan was *"We will make a country to live equally well."*

They extolled Kim Il Sung (northern Korea leader) and crushed Rhee, Syng Man (southern Korea leader). Most of the attendants were farmers.

They were so tired after their farm work that many of the attendants were drowsing when a partisan was giving a long and loud winded speech. They also taught a few songs; General Kim Il Sung, The Morning Shine and The Revolutionary Song.

I was a good soloist in our school and they stood me on the platform to sing the song of General Kim, Il Sung at the beginning of the meeting.

The meetings were on and on but the people could not be absent from the meetings because they were afraid of being treated as "Reactionary elements".

The communists once occupied a place and they purged the educated, the rich and the religious because they were the ones who were not obedient and reactionary to the communism.

In our school we had a meeting every morning before the class and another one after school in the afternoon.

We had a unique program called "Self Criticism Hour".

At that time we had to confess our wrong doings and the class criticized the wrong doers standing on the platform.

I once stood up to confess my wrong doing on the platform of our class. Actually, I confessed it to my cousin already, but my childish mind made myself stand up there again and I was criticized by my class;

In that country village the chimney of the house was not high.

I could reach to the chimney pot. My second cousin at my next door was heating up in the kitchen. A childish mischief of mine occurred to make fun of my cousin and I took off my jacket and covered the chimney pot. Naturally the smoke was reversed to the fuel hole where she was burning firewood and I heard her severely coughing and running out of the kitchen. I ran away without her knowing.

Once we had a voting for the premier.

Kim, IL Sung was the sole candidate.

The poll was situated in our school playground.

It was surrounded with wide cloth like a fence and two boxes were laid. One was white in color and the other one was black.

Those who supported Kim, IL Sung should have gone to the white box to cast the ballot. Those who did not support him should have gone to the black box. They called it *The Secret Poll*.

At that time I was the third grade.

EXODUS

We got on the train toward the south to depart from the northern Korea to the southern Korea late summer in 1946.

It was very hot and very humid like late summer.

The journey was desperate and dangerous.

My little newborn sister, Young Sun, cried out distinctively in the train. Her crying sounded loud and clear.

It was quite natural that her crying should have discomforted passengers. I could see a few faces being frowned.

At that time a gentleman said loudly, *"Wow! Her voice is great. She will make a good singer someday."* Unbelievably her crying stopped.

The miracle continued until we reached near to the 38th parallel which had divided Korea into two.

My father had already been once to Seoul secretly to find out the route how to escape to the south.

In 1946 the northern authority did not shoot the refugees yet.

They just urged the refugees to go back to their home towns.

We pretended to pay a visit to a relative home near the 38th parallel for the family's wedding.

It could not be a reasonable excuse because our appearance in traveling outfit was telling our moving to the south.

A guard called us as suspects and we were detained in a room of a house with a little mama and papa grocery store at the roadside.

We were caught early in the morning.

We were allowed to buy something to eat from the store.

Some others also were detained at the same place and allowed to buy something to eat and drink as well.

My little brother was whispering to my father,

"Let's escape through the back door."

The guard was smiling at him. Young-Yi was 4 years old going on to 5 year old boy and I was going on to 10 year old one.

It was getting to the evening before sunset.

The guard released us with the others and told us nicely to go back to our home towns. We came out of the detention room and pretended to go back to our town. On the way back toward the north my father found a house by the street to stay overnight.

Next morning my father was informed that the owner of the house had been guiding the defectors to the south. The house owner held us one week at his house giving us cautions of the guards at the border line. He charged for room and board fees day by day. On the seventh night I could hear my father telling the house owner that he did have spent all the money he had and he could not pay for the room and board any more saying *"You must guide our family to the south tonight."*

We were guided to the south by that night.

It was as dark as pitch. We had to prostrate ourselves a few times by the order of the guide on the way to the south.

As we heard some people's muttering and we were about to prostrate ourselves the guide said, *"Finally we made it."* and

"We are now in the south."

I was so happy that I jumped into the air of darkness. But alas!

I jumped in the air and fell into the pond. In the pitch-darkness I was calling my father and he plunged into the pond toward my voice calling.

I was saved by my father in the pitch-darkness.

We went in a house and so many people were already there.

It was so late over midnight. We were so tired that each one had to find a place to sleep as my father instructed. There was no space to lie down. All the people were sleeping sitting on the floor leaning one another. It was quite a sight to see a woman sleeping putting her cheek to a strange man's cheek without knowing it.

Next morning we walked along with the people to the Tong Young railroad station to get the train to Seoul. The numerous refugees were already waiting for the train.

THE SOUTHERN KOREA

The atmosphere of the southern Korea was quite different from it of the northern Korea. No one bothered any one by calling meetings. They did not rally the workers. I could not hear any catchphrase – *"We will make a country to live equally well."*

Everyone was just busy to support oneself or his family.

It was also a poor country but a free country.

I could hear the Communists were also implicitly acting in southern Korea.

They tried to destroy the social orders in many schemes and means like strikes. The communists were so defiant, resentful and destructive in the southern Korea.

On August 15, 1948 the Republic of Korea was founded in the southern Korea.

The first president was Rhee, Syng man. The new government began to establish the social order. The communist riot in the southern Korea gradually went to decay by the new government police force and the army.

Tae Pyoung Primary School

I was admitted in the 4th grade of Tae Pyeong (means perfect peace) primary school. On the first day of my attending school I was introduced to the class by the teacher in charge of the 4th grade class.

Surprisingly I was requested to sing a song after my greeting to the class. Dubiously the teacher told the class to close the windows and then asked me to sing a song of the northern Korea.

I was puzzled what to do because I had been told not to sing any northern Korean songs any more in Seoul by my father.

I was hesitating. The teacher asked me again saying *"It is OK. No problem."* After a little while of hesitation I began to sing the Shining Morning. As soon as I finished the song he asked me to sing another one. I sang 'General Kim Il Sung'. At that time my knowledge about the communism was totally lack.

When I became to be aware well of communism after Korean War I heard the teacher had gone to the northern Korea. I was sorry for him. He must have been influenced by Karl Marxism.

In Korea they say among friends, *"If a young man in twenties is not fascinated by Karl Marx he is rather dull but if he does not get out of Karl Marx influence after twenties he is a real fool.*

Dear children, I think I had a little romance in this primay school.

I was the monitor (president) of our class. Choi, Young Sook was the monitor of the other class. She was smart and pretty. When we had an exam she often obtained a better record than I did and she won the first place from time to time in our 6th grade classes.

Whenever she came to our class I was just inexplicably happy and my class friends made fun of me, "Here comes the future wife of Young George." Once I was invited to her house and her mother showed me boundless hospitality to me, which I cannot forget. After our graduation from the school I heard she moved to Daegu, KyoengSangBuk-Do.

"THE ATOMIC BOMB OF LOVE"

The ideological conflict between the right wing and the left wing was here and there in the southern Korea. And yet a big rebellion of the communists occurred in two cities on April 19, 1948;

In Yeosoo and Sooncheon in Cholla Nam-Do; <u>South Korean army 14 regiment force rebellion</u> was the big misery; Communists stirred the people up to revolt and killed many innocent citizens in those two cities.

The so-called "<u>Bbaljjisan</u>" communist guerilla fighters killed so many innocent people brutally and heinously as they were retreating into the Jiri Mountains due to the counterattack of our Korean National Defense forces.

I think I must not skip this story to my children;

A young insurgent killed <u>Dong-In</u> and <u>Dong-Shin</u>, two sons of Rev. <u>Sohn,</u> Yang Won. He was a pastor of great faith in Christianity. We came to call him "The Atomic Bomb of Love".

He was the man of love who forgave the killer of his own two sons and adopted him as his son. He was really a man of faith.

It is our great blessing to have such an ancestor of faith.

He was a man of fullness of Holy Spirit.

May God bless the land of Korea eternally because of him!

Joyful Sunday-School

I would say that Shin Dang Dong Je IL Presbyterian Church was my mother church. It was a small church located at Yak Su Dong in Seoul City.

Sunday-school students were less than seventy in my memory.

My personality was molded, formed and built in this Sunday-school. Listening to the bible stories was my greatest happiness.

Singing hymns made me hilarious.

I sang a solo or acted as an actor in a few Christmas dramas in Christmas seasons.

Singing Christmas Carols visiting the church members' homes before the dawn on Christmas Day early morning was the unspeakable joy and happiness.

It was cold but we did not care for it.

Almost every home treated us with dduckkuk prepared warmly.

As I am reflecting the days of Sunday-school I find myself becoming already a happy boy in no time.

I remember it was one hot day of summer in 1949.

A few boys of our village seemed so infuriated. I asked them the reason. Their story was as follows: They were on the way to church. Some boys in the next village to the church barred our boys from going to church. Our boys were inferior in strength. They were just returning home. I gathered more boys and pursued them. I pursued after the tallest guy and he ran into his house. I kept pursuing after him into his house. His mother was at the porch and she asked me,

"What's the matter?"

I explained how he hindered our boys' going to church. But alas! Right away I recognized her. She was my teacher of the kindergarten that I had graduated from in northern Korea (Kwang Myung Yuchiwon – Bright Light Kindergarten).

The next day she visited our home to see my mother with a big basket of fruit to apologize for the incident.

When I became a high student I became a member of the High School Choir in this church. I was a member of the base part. This happened after the Korean War.

At that time I met my best and lifetime friend, Kim Jung Woo.

He was a member of the tenor part.

I want to put off my writing about the happiest reminiscence of my high school period and the church life until the next chance of my writing.

On June 25, 1950 the civil war carried off our happiness.

KOREAN WAR

I was in Junior high when the Korean War broke out.

Korean War brought us speechless tragedy.

Early in the morning on Sunday June 25, 1950 the communist northern Korean army, so called "Red Army" invaded southern Korea with the Russian made tanks at the head of aggression.

The machine-gunning of the fighters of the Red Army was continued over the headquarters of the southern Korean Army in Yong San district. Any air battle was not seen because the southern Korean army did not have any fighters.

In three days Seoul City was under the Red Army control because southern Korea was not prepared at all for war.

While the Red Army occupied Seoul City the recorded tape was playing and broadcasting on and on at the Seoul radio station;

"My dear people, our Korean National Defense Soldiers are fighting bravely and well. They will defeat the Red Army soon. Please do not be afraid and panic at all"

It was the prerecorded voice of the president Rhee Syngman.

Treacherously to the people, the president Rhee Syngman with the government cabinet members had already escaped to Busan,

a southern tip harbor city, the second largest city of southern Korea.

My father, mother, I, my brother Young Yi and sister Young Sun lived under the Red Army occupation for three months.

During the miserable three months our life was the continuous fighting with hunger and hiding and keeping ourselves away from the communists' sight as much as possible.

The president Rhee Syngman asked for help to the United Nations. The UN united forces' landing operation at Inchon harbor under the supreme commander general Douglas McArthur was successfully achieved on September 28, 1950 and southern Korea was freed from the communist control. The UN united forces thrust out the Red Army away up to the Abrok River which was the border line between Korea and China.

Unfortunately the victory did not last long.

On January 4, 1951 we had to flee southward to Busan to take a shelter because the Chinese "human-wave tactics" began; The Chinese communist army of 1,000,000 (allegedly) infantrymen crossed the border and advanced southward beating gongs.

At that time we decided to leave Seoul to go to Busan.

Knowing it afterwards, our family members could have been killed by the communists if the UN forces landing operation had been delayed one day because we had come down from the north in opposition to the communist regime. The list of mass killing the defectors from the northern Korea was found after the communist retreat in the local district office. This was the information of word

from mouth to mouth.

It took one week by train for us to get to Busan, a south tip city because the train was allowed to be in motion without interruption of the trains with war supplies toward the north front line. It takes only four hours now by bullet train from Seoul to Busan.

UNCLE JAE KOOK

The Red-army occupied Seoul City in three days after war beginning and a few weeks passed. Uncle Jae Kook (wae-samchon, my mother's younger brother) who was a senior student of high school was captured by the Red-army conscripting officer on the street and drafted into the Red-army. He was on the way home from his friend's house.

My wae-halmoni came to know about his being drafted from his friend. Actually it was a guess of his friend at that time. The guess was backed up with the rumor afloat.

My wae-halmoni waited and waited for him without knowing his being drafted into the Red-army. She began to call on his friends one by one from the next day of his conscription. After three day search she came to meet the friend who had met wae-samchon on that day of his being captured on the street. This is how they guessed that he had been captured on the way home from his house.

This is the story that I heard from my uncle when I was in the high school period; it was hot and muggy day. He was being dragged to the north in a line with other draftees being guarded by the Red-army soldiers.

As they reached the hill top of Miari Gogae all of sudden some captures began to run away. He said that only a few captures might have been successful in escaping because the warning gun firing started soon and the escaping was stopped. My uncle also watched for a chance to escape, but he did not have any luck. Therefore he walked and walked toward the north almost without rest. They could rest only when the UN fighters were flying over their heads. So, they were so glad to see the fighters. On the contrary the Red-army soldiers were dreadfully afraid of them. He had no idea how many days had passed.

At the dawn He suddenly came to recognize the buildings along the road. He was aware of himself in Jin Nam Po where he was living before having moved to Seoul. He was pleased to see around the places for a moment. Immediately He began to confirm all the streets and alleys where he was running around with friends. He felt some kind of confidence. He could figure out all the alleys. He made up his mind to escape. Fortunately the soldiers' caution also became very loose because they might think the captures would not escape because of geographic ignorance and the distance from Seoul.

At last he got to the spot to hide himself swiftly into the alley.
He ran and ran through the zigzag alleys.
He said the soldiers might not have been aware of my escape for quite a while. When he came to think he ran away far enough from the escaping place he stopped to think how to go to the south without any failure. He decided to go along the railroad instead of highway. It was not difficult to find the railroad for he would play on the railway before with friends.

The long walk along the railroad toward the south began.

He walked mostly at night to avoid people's eye. He moved cautiously hiding as best he could during the day. He took something to eat from the farms at night. He was in constant feet pain and extreme hunger. After a trek of over two months ever since his being captured he could reach Seoul, but he was afraid extremely of being recaptured again. As soon as he saw some Peoples' army (Red army) soldiers on the streets he could not move further. He reflected that being hungry was the most difficult suffering. Finally he could come home through all sorts of hardships and suffering many privations.

REFUGEE LIFE

Our refugee life began first at an imo's house (an aunt's house) in Busan. Imo was one of the second cousins of my mother. Her husband had been working for the national railroad administration from 1947. Her house was not big enough to occupy ten people together.

Imo and her husband were generous for us to live with them for two months until we moved to Kim Hae as soon as my father got the job in Kim Hae.

A fifteen year old peddler

I guessed our crowded life in Imo's house had consumed about one month. Of course, my parents must have worried about earning a living. I requested my mother 1000 Hwan - the monetary unit at that time – and she handed it to me without any question.

I went to the maker of Yeot in the market place which was a kind of Korean sweet candies made from rice. I purchased ggayeots for 1000 Hwan. They gave me fifteen ggayeots for 1000 Hwan.

A yeot was the plain 4" long stick candy, but a ggayeot was the one coated with parched sesame seeds on it. I cut an American GI ration box into two by a half to carry them and displayed them in it.

I walked along the street and offered to buy ggayeot to the people gathered here and there. I charged 100 Hwan for a piece. It didn't take long to sell them out. I bought another fifteen ggayeots for 1000 Hwan again. I started to walk along the different street.

I could sell them out before dusk and came back home with the profit of 1000 Hwan.

After a few days of peddling along the streets I happened to run along the pier. So many ships were anchored at the dock. I found five or six people were gathered in a ship to play cards. I bustled on board and offered to buy ggayeot to them. They welcomed me and asked me to bring more. My peddling of ggayeots gave me five or six thousand Hwan of profit a day. It was really fun.

One night, my father called me and spoke highly of my work and said to stop it. He smiled at me saying, *"It is not a good thing for a young man like you to have fun in making money."*

Life at Pyung Jin Burak

It was a small beautiful village situated between a big orchard surrounded by the fence of tangerine trees and a river - actually a part of the big irrigation canal. My father found a job in a mess hall in American GI barracks.

Korean War lasted for three years.

We were blessed to eat enough and dressed neatly because of our parents' hard work even though we were in a strange and unknown places during the miserable war.

Thanks to the Lord!

His grace reminded me the story of the widow's oil at Shunem
(2 Kings 4).

We attended Pyeong Gang (peace) Presbyterian Church which had a good Sunday school.

I was baptized by an American missionary in 1952.

In 2003 I paid a visit to the church and I had a chance to read the session record of the church. It was my great pleasure to confirm my baptism looking up the date of baptism in the session record.

Fortunately I could start to study at Dae Kwang Middle School. The school was a Christian school established by Dr. and Rev. Han Kyung-Chik to whom The Templeton Prize was given in 2007.

My father started business with two weaving machines as soon as he quit the job of GI mess hall.

My brother Young Kwan was born on December 17, 1952.

Young Kwan's birth place was Pyeongjin Boorak, Daesari, Grak-Myun, Kim Hae Kun, Kyeong Sang Nam Do (a part of Busan City now).

Young Kwan is now in Philippines as a missionary.

His American name is John Lee. Pastor John Lee and his wife Kyu Sook have been already over three years in Philippines.

Memorable Sunday school in refuge life

Pyeong Jin Boorak was the name of the little beautiful village.

Less than forty farm households were gathered together at a corner of the broad and wide Kim-Hae plain which was the biggest plain in Korea. Most of rice fields were watered by the irrigation system.

A not wide long alley was running parallel along the tangerine fence of the orchard. The houses were embraced by the bamboo trees along the alley which led to the main roadway.

I would get up early in the morning and sweep the alley along the tangerine fence to the main roadway. I met the elders of the village going out to their farms. I greeted them with a smile and with courtesy. *"Anyunghi Jumushutseumnigga"*---Have you slept well, Sir? ---Good morning, Sir?

or *"Geo Noasimnigga"* – Hi there, Sir - This expression was a peculiar expression of greeting in this region.

This greeting particularly interested me.

It was my daily early morning job.

They were so humble and peaceful.

They must have seen me going to church.

My attitude became to their liking.

"The boy from Seoul is different,"

This word was spread out in the village.

They urged their ch to go to church with me.

As I mentioned above the Pyeong Gang Presbyterian Church had a good Sunday school. I remember I took so many children to the Sunday school on Sundays.

It was regretful that I found out their attendance to church had stopped after our family moving back to Seoul. A few girls were still attending the church though.

Junior High Period

The most of my Junior High period was the life of refugee in Kim-Hae (now a part of Busan City) during the Korean War. Our school was located at the mountainside of Mount Chun-Ma looking down the Pacific Ocean in Busan City which is a harbor city.

The school structures were the tents framed by wood panels which were obtained from war supplies. The teachers and the students were poor in the unbalanced nutrition but eager and earnest in teaching and learning.

Whenever I look back on the Junior High period I feel guilty due to a happening (we called it "Strike" at that time) of the Chinese writing class; Frankly speaking it was not an easy subject to study.

It was my immature act to the teacher of Chinese writing class.

I said to the class, *"I want to refuse the mid-term test of Chinese writing class because his teaching is not good enough for us to understand. We require a better skill of teaching for us to understand better."*

We had two classes in the second grade of Junior High - the eighth grade in American way. My claim was accepted by the both two classes.

Probably most of the classmates had the same troubles as I had.

I did not go to the other class, but my claim was relayed to the other class too and accepted.

As soon as the examination of Chinese writing subject began I wrote only my name on the test-paper and submitted it on the teaching desk and came out of the class.

Naturally my classmates followed after me in awkward manners.

I heard the strike was stopped in the other class because the teacher who presided over the examination became aware of it in advance. He caught and severely slapped on the cheek of the student who was handing in the test-paper firstly.

Next day I and another classmate were summoned to the teacher who was in charge of discipline and academic affairs.

I was inquired why I led the "strike".

I explained, *"I come to school in all train-ride. It takes me two or three hours. Sometimes I arrived at the school at lunch time due to the war supplies train. I've got frustrated by the Chinese writing class experiencing it unsatisfactorily after my long trip to School."*

The other student who was summoned was also an honor student.

The teacher of Chinese writing subject was not seen since then.

Because of me - an immature student, the poor teacher lost his job in refugee life during the difficult time of war.

How hard his life was! His family! It was not what I wanted.

What did I earn through it?

THE FIRST FIGHT

It was an English class.

The teacher asked a question about an irregular verb 'cut';

"He cut the tree." It was a conjugation matter.

"The present form is cut and the past form is also cut."

"How do you figure out the tense of this cut?" The class was silent.

I knew the answer, but I did not answer because I felt sorry for answering for every question by myself. After a while of silence the teacher pointed out me to answer.

I answered, "It is a past tense form." "Why do you think so?"

The teacher asked the question in return.

I answered, "If the tense is present it should be <u>cuts</u> because the subject is third person, single and present tense we must add 's' to the verb."

"Right precisely."

"He cut the tree." should be "He cuts the tree if it is present."

"The grammar tells that the subject is the third person, single and the tense is present we must add 's' to the verb."

Regretfully a sarcastic sound was simultaneously heard in silence.

"Having known the answer he should have answered earlier."

A guy reproached me for not answering at the beginning when the question was asked the first.

His sarcastic remark was not the first time.

He had done this kind of sarcastic remark a few times before.

I had understood his personality of jealousy, but I had decided not to tolerate him for this time.

After class I approached him and said to him to meet outside silently without other students being noticed.

We had a big fistic fight. We came back to the class late after we had cleaned our hands and faces thoroughly.

I remember his name. I do not know why he was not with us when we became the third grade (ninth grade).

A STUDENT'S TESTIMONY

We were studying in the tent classrooms pitched on the hillside of Mt. Chun-ma in Busan during the refuge life.

All the students of the junior high and the senior high were gathered together in the morning before the study at the outdoor seats arranged in tiers on the hillside. It was the worship hour before the classes, which was a routine of our school as a Christian school.

Especially in that morning there was a student's testimony that I can never forget in my life. He was a senior. He had come down just several months before from the north. As I told you before our school had been established by Dr. & Rev. Han, Kyung Jik with the Christian refugees from the northern Korea at that time.

For this reason the majority of the students were composed of the Christians from the north like me.

He started his testimony; he was coming down toward the south around January 4, 1951-retreat due to the Chinese soldiers' joining the war. After a good while of walking he found himself behind the Chinese battle line. The front line was way ahead of him.

He was just walking continuously. "Hands up" a shouting was heard. He was caught by the North Korean Red-Army soldiers.

He found four other men captured in the same platoon.

The officer was accompanied with a soldier and the prisoners were taken to the mountain at dusk.

The officer ordered to line up the prisoners in one line widthwise.

The student of witness was allowed to say his last words before death. He asked to allow him to sing a hymn.

He was allowed to sing a hymn.

The moon was beaming down between the pine trees.

His song was started:

"The bright road to the heaven is before me.
Even though I am in hardship with a lot of sorrow
The brightness of heavenly glory scatters the dark shadow.
I see always the light relying on His elaboration."

His singing hymn continued to the third stanza.

The officer said, "I myself will put them to death."

Simultaneously he pulled out his pistol and started shooting.

The witness said, "He was thinking he was dying."

Naturally all fell down with the sound of gunfire except the officer.

But alas! He found himself alive with other three prisoners.

The officer called over them and told them to run away.

The Red-army soldier who accompanied with the officer was lying down dead alone there.

ARMISTICE AGREEMENT

The armistice agreement between U.N. Forces and North Korea (China) was signed on July 27, 1953. Our refugee life of three years in Kim-Hae ended and we came back home in Seoul.

Korean War ceased with the death of over 3,200,000 people.

Korea had been squeezed out under the Japanese Control.
Japanese had exploited Koreans as much as they could.
Even Korean mountains had been stripped for the World War II.

Having one misfortune on top of another, Korea became extremely poor to be placed in the poorest country but one in Africa.
Korean people became ground down to be able to scarcely breathe.
South Korea was devastated by three year war and nothing was left but poverty. It seemed hopeless.

I recall what Rev. Billy Graham said in the revival meeting at Yeouido square in Seoul, Korea in 1973; "I woke up in Canada by birds' chirpings. I woke up in Japan by workmen's chatters, I woke up in Korea by the church bell calling for dawn prayer meetings.

Yes, our Korean Christians cried out to the Lord in the dawn prayer meetings. Every church had the dawn prayer meeting throughout the country. Every morning of 6 days a week except Sundays the dawn prayer meetings have been continuing without cease until this day.

Our Lord, Our God, Our Savior answered our prayers.
Korea is now set in the tenth place economically in the world.
Right after Korean War an Englishman said, *"It is much the same Korea gets economically developed as a rose grows on the pile of garbage."*

The country had been devastated by three year war.
Yes, it was a thing impossible in human's eye-view to restore it.
It was entirely God's grace.
I want you to recall the word: *"The Valley of Dry Bones" in Chapter 37 of Ezekiel; "The Sovereign Lord says to these bones: I will make breath enter you, and you will come to life. I will attach tendons to you and make flesh come upon you and cover you with skins; I will put breath in you, and you will come to life. Then you will know that I am the Lord."--- Ezk-37:5-6.*

In the Valley of Dry Bones of Korea many a many roses miraculously came into bloom spiritually and materially.

"God has chosen the foolish things of the world to put to shame the wise. God has chosen the weak things of the world to put to shame the things which are mighty."--- 1 Cor. 1:27.

Hallelujah! Praises to the Lord! Glory and Thanks to the Lord!

The Lord has been blessed us through the sufferings.

That is why we should not be afraid of sufferings.

We should rejoice expecting His blessings beyond the sufferings. *"We rejoice in the hope of the glory of God. Not only so, but we also rejoice in our sufferings, because we know that suffering produces perseverance; perseverance, character; and character, hope." –Rome 5:3,4.*

Figure rough
<u>Translation of the above diagram by date.</u>

6.25.1950	**Invasion of North Communist Red Army**
9.02.1950	**the farthest invasion line to the south of The Red Army**
9.15.1950	**Landing Operation at Inchon harbor of General MacArthur**
9.28. 1950	**Retaking of Seoul City by the UN united army**
10.19.1950	**Occupation of Pyeong Yang City**
10.25.1950	**Chinese Red Army intervention**
11.01.1950	**March onward to the Abrok River**
11.25.1950	**the farthest advance line to the north of the UN united army**
01.08.1951	**the farthest invasion line to the south of Chinese Red Army**
6.18.1953	**release of anti-Communist prisoners of war**
7.27.1953	**signing of armistice agreement**

MOTHER WAS GREAT

During the Korean War our family lost none of our family members nor relatives. The Korean War took lives of 3,200,000.

The food shortage was serious during the war.

The Red-army entered Seoul City so quickly that we could not escape to the south.

We believed the radio broadcast which had been recorded and was being on air repeatedly.

When we found out it was the pre-recorded broadcast the Han River iron bridge and iron railway bridge had been already exploded and the refuge route was blocked - At that time there were two bridges only over the Han River and now thirty ones.

We had to stay under the communist control for three months until

General McArthur's Inchon Landing Operation was successfully achieved on September 25, 1950 and Seoul City was retaken on September 28, 1950.

The food problem was serious during the three months occupied by North Korean Red-army. My father was operating a small cotton mill and we had some textile fabrics in stock.

My mother went to the farm villages and exchanged them with rice, some grains and vegetables. The aggravation of food shortage forced a lot of citizens of Seoul to seek for food. I heard it made a long line of people seeking provisions on the street;

People carrying food on their heads, people carrying with handcarts, with pushcarts, with carriages by a cow.

Woe is to my mother!

She was one of them carrying food on her head for us (me, Young Yi and Young Sun including my father). My father was hiding himself in a secret place to avoid being drafted into the red army work. By dint of our mother's hard work we were not hungry.

She was the mother of three children at that time.

She told us always that she was neither difficult nor weary.

Who said, *"Woman is weak, but mother is strong."*?

시 Poem

어머니에게 드립니다
*1969년 어머니날에 즈음하여
미국에서 한국에 계신 어머니에게

어머니!
당신은 희생의 모태입니다.
내 적은 생명이 당신 속에서 자랄 때부터
나는 당신의 생명을 먹었습니다.
내 눈속에 빛이 처음 들어 오던 날
나는 세상에서 가장 큰 고통을 주었습니다.

어머니!
당신은 나의 식탁입니다.
솔로몬의 식탁보다 더 큰 식탁입니다.
우유빛 나는 당신 품에 안길 때면
세상에 부러운 딴 음식이 없었습니다.
당신의 품은 나의 식탁입니다.

어머니!
당신은 나의 침실입니다.
홍단이불 금단이불 공작 수놓은 이불보다
젖냄새 나는 당신 품이 좋았습니다.
거기에는 아무런 위험도 없었습니다.
밉고 고운 자식이 없었습니다.
당신은 나의 침실입니다.

어머니!
당신은 나의 노리터입니다.
거기에는 파란 잔디가 깔렸고
손발과 머리가 상할 아무 것도 없어서
어느 놀이터보다 좋았습니다.
당신의 품은 나의 놀이터입니다.

어머니!
당신은 나의 산 교훈입니다.

Dear my mother
*At the time of Mother's Day in 1969
from America to my mother in Korea.

Mother!
You are the womb of the sacrifice.
I ate your life from the time of
my little life growing in you.
On the day as the light came into my eyes
I gave you the greatest pain in the world.

Mother!
You are my table.
It is bigger than Solomon's one.
When being embraced in your bosom
I envy no other food in the world.
Your bosom is my table.

Mother!
You are my bed room.
I prefer your milk-smelling bosom to
an silk blanket, a coverlet embroidered
peacock with gold. No danger was there.
There was no hateful or pretty child.
You are my bed room.

Mother!
You are my playground.
It was covered with green lawn.
I loved it more than any other place 'cause
it has no harmful things to hurt hands, feet
and head. Your bosom is my playground.

Mother!
You are my living lesson.

당신의 말을 들으면 틀림 없었고
당신이 하라는대로 하면 실수가 없었습니다.
당신의 참으심은 십자가
당신의 사랑은 십자가의 사랑을
보여 주셨습니다.

어머니!
당신은 나의 웃음입니다.
당신이 옆에만 있어도 좋았습니다.
당신이 웃으면 더 좋았습니다.
내 얼굴에 웃음을 보시려고
당신은 어두운 곳에서 우셨습니다.

어머니!
당신은 나의 안식처입니다.
당신이 계시면 온기가 돌았습니다
엄동설한 긴긴 밤에도
당신만 있으면 추위를 몰랐습니다.

어머니!
당신은 나의 의사입니다.
목이 타도록 열이 올라도
깨어지듯 머리가 아파도
당신의 손만 와 닿으면 난 것 같았습니다.
"내 손이 약손이야요, 내 손이 약손이야요"
나는 잠이 들어도
당신은 밤을 새웠습니다.
하나님이 어떤 날
천사에게 심부름을 시켰답니다.
세상에서 가장 아름다운 것을 가져 오라고
처음에는 꽃을 가져 왔고
다음에는 어린아이의 웃음을 가져 왔고
세번째는 어머니의 사랑을 가벼 왔더랍니다.
세월이 지났더랍니다.
꽃은 시들어지고
아기의 웃음은 근심으로 찡그러졌지만
어머니의 사랑은 변한이 없더랍니다.

Listening to you was unfailing.
Your words resulted in no mistakes.
Your endurance meant
the perseverance of the Cross.
Your love showed the love of the Cross.

Mother!
You are my smile.
Your being beside me did please me.
I was happier when you smile.
You wept in the darkness to see smiles
on my face.

Mother!
You are my place to rest.
Warmth spreads out instantly on
your presence. Even if it was a long
and cold night I did not feel cold
as only you were with me.

Mother!
You are my doctor of medicine.
Even my throat burning with high fever
Even my head hurting as if crashing,
Pain seemed gone on your hand touching.
"My hand is of medicine. My hand is of
medicine" Though I'd gone to sleep
You stayed up all night.
One day God sent an angel on an errand
to bring the most beautiful things to Him.
Firstly, he brought a flower.
Secondly, he brought a baby's smile.
Thirdly, he brought mother's love.
As time passed by flower withered,
Baby's smile frowned with anxiety though,
Mother's love remained unchanged.

A Proof of Being Chosen

It was a stormy night.

It was pitch-dark.

Rolls of thunder were heard in the distance.

The rain like chicken droppings was falling down roughly from the sky.

My mother was gathering up her late mother-in-law's belongings in her room. Some brand-new and rather expensive clothes were full in the chest.

My mother handed out some clothes to the wife of her husband's younger brother saying, *"You wear these."*

"Anio(No), Hyungnim(big sister), I do not want to wear them."

She added, *"I'm afraid late mother-in-law's ghost might be hanging on them."*

My mother said, *"There is no such thing like ghost."*

"If you don't want them I will wear them or give them to somebody else."

My mother collected all the old stuffs which had belonged to her mother-in-law. She took the stuffs with her and went out of the room to throw them away.

To the surprise she took out the altar which had been used to hold memorial service for the ancestors and carried out of the room to throw it away.

My father's younger brother's wife was trembling with fear.

My mother was acting swiftly without fear.

She looked rather free from something.

She threw away all the stuffs into the river which was flooded by heavy rainstorms in the pitch darkness.

The thunder crashed and rumbled and the lightning flashed.

My mother was not well educated.

My mother was not aware of the Lord.

My mother never heard of the name of Jesus.

Probably she might have heard from her younger sister (Jae Hyun), but could not have kept it in mind because she was always busy in mind.

How can you explain her courage?

God's elect of her only can explain it.

She merely did not know Him then.

I believe it is a proof of her having been chosen by God when she was not aware of the Lord.

HIGH SCHOOL PERIOD

Private English Class

It was a peaceful period after the truce.

I had good friends - Jung Wu, Bong Ryeol, and a few others.

We used to enjoy a camp life during the summer vacations on the beautiful and clean sands which had been formed on the riverside of the Han River on the opposite side of the present Walker Hill Hotel.

Regretfully, the sands is not there any longer due to the city development.

The U.S. Army continuously stationed in Korea after the truce.

We had English classes (English reader, English grammar and English composition) as our regular subjects from Junior high to high school and just reader in the college in Korea, but our English speaking ability was extremely poor.

A private English class started with ten friends including me at Deok Young's house in Yong San area. A first lieutenant of U.S. army was invited as our teacher who was serving in the barracks of the eighth army headquarters in Yong San. We met three days a week after school.

Our English speaking ability was improved practically.

We learned also the Star Spangled Banner - the National Anthem of the United States of America at that time.

Knuckle Buster

Our school was holding an athletic meeting on the anniversary of the opening of our school. One incident happened at the entrance of the main gate of our school on that day of October in 1955.

I was busy in conducting visitors to the visitors' seats with two other students' Discipline Staffs at the main gate.

The playground was being filled with students, visitors and parents. Visitors were rushing in through the gate as the opening time of the meeting was approaching. All of a sudden, I saw a disorderly student wearing an armband of the Discipline Staff was standing at the gate instead of the designated Staff. I went to him and said, *"Why are you here?" "Go back to your seat."*

He stroke a blow on my face. It happened in a flash.

Almost simultaneously I looked around.

Some visitors seemed to have seen the incident.

I pulled him behind the guard office building and started to give him continuous blows on his face until he was knocked down.

I was in a rage because I came to think he made our Christian school shameful among the visitors.

That guy challenged me to fight again after the athletic meeting.
"If we fight in the school things are unfavorable for me and let's fight outside the school." This was the guy's suggestion.

This news spread out quickly to the classmates.
This guy's name was A.B. who used to carry a knife in a specially made pocket in the trouser leg. That was why everyone was afraid of him. This fighting made them so interested for he was known as a good fighter and I was known as a model student.
That fight was furiously performed being watched by tens of onlookers-on outside the school.

Four days were passing by since the fight.
That guy was being absent from school over four days.
Also this day he was absent.
I was summoned to the office of teachers after school on Thursday. The teacher in charge of our class said, *"Young George, you and I will pay a visit to B.C. today."*
It was the teacher's duty to visit the student who were absent from school over three days. I had to accompany with him for I was the monitor of our class.

In those days telephones were for the rich only.
Most of families did not have any telephones.

Because of our sudden visit to A. B. without any notification he seemed precisely flustered looking at me for he was massaging around his black eyes with an egg which had been bruised by the fight against me.
In a few days from that day of our visit he started to attend school.
I am afraid we did not do anything discreetly for reconciliation.
Days just passed so.

The Students' Discipline Staffs: the fourth from right/me

FLEXIBILITY OF A RULE

This is also a story of my high school period.

I was the class president (monitor). As the class begins the teacher stands on the platform to receive the salutation from the students. As soon as the teacher stands on the platform I give a command - *"Attention"* and I make a military salute saying, *"Ready to study"*. This salute has to be done in each class. This regulation took effect from the elementary school to the high school. In the colleges they did not have this regulation.

It was the time of ending of juniors.

I was asked by the teacher in charge of our class to help him to arrange the report cards of our class. Of course I gave him some help. It was my privilege to work with the matter which might incur to be blamed because it was the confidential work of papers.

After all the report cards were arranged the teacher picked out two cards which should stay back in the same grade class due to failing marks.

It was the moment for the two guys to move up to the senior or not.

He picked up one guy's card and said, *"This guy's human nature is pretty good and I will let him move up to the senior class."*

He picked up the other card and said, *"This guy's human nature is not good enough to be a senior."* He added, *"This guy is really out of range."*

When I became a senior I could not see the latter guy any longer in the school.

According to the hearsay information he was attending a certain high school.

I met him at a certain church many decades later.

He was an elder of that church.

ACT AS A MIDWIFE

In school I was in two year grade below than my same age bracket due to the moving down to the southern Korea and Korean War.

It was a month away from the high school graduation.

When I was entering home from school and about to say to my mother, *"Mother, I am home now from school"* I heard severe groan.

I hurried into my mother's room. She was going through the pain of labor. I still remember what she said to me;

"I am embarrassed to see you."

It was her single pathetic word to me when she found out her pregnancy of Hae Sun, the fifth child of her, my little sister.

She instructed me what to do calmly.

I became busy in the kitchen boiling water and sanitizing the scissors.

My mother was calm and swift in her experienced mother instinct.

I held the baby in my own hands.

I cut the navel cord according to her instruction.

On January 28, 1957 my youngest sister Hae Sun (Sunny) was born.

I was going on 20 years old.

My job of midwife was successful.

My mother was healthy and my darling sister was healthy.

Sunny is living in Arizona now.

4. 19. REVOLUTION

The revolution was led by college students and high school students.

On April 19, 1960, when so called 4.19. Revolution broke out I was a student of the college of Business, Yon-Sei University, Seoul, Korea. The demonstration parade of the students of Yon-Sei University was passing by in front of the government building – the government-general building built by Japanese, which was demolished during the period of President Kim, Young-Sam (1993-1998). I personally opposed his decision of demolishing the building. I assert the disgrace is also a history. The policemen started to fire guns toward our students and we instantly prostrated ourselves. A sharp scream was heard from the front of the parade: *"Students are injured."* I saw some students bleeding and being carried away to the rear of the parade. Lee, Han Yeol, a student of Yon-Sei University was killed at that time and many students were wounded.

In the general election on May 20, 1954 the Liberal Party of President Syngman Rhee secured 99 seats in the National Assembly and became the number one party.

The party started to aim to secure the optimum number (two thirds) of assemblymen for the constitutional amendment. They subsumed the independent assemblymen and secured 137 seats to amend the constitution that restricts three term election so that they may give lifetime power to Syngman Rhee.

To prolong the power of Syngman Rhee they rigged a fraudulent election on March 15, 1960.

This rigged election caused 4.19. Revolution by the students.

This brought the consequence of the step-down of Syngman Rhee from his power.

KOREA AWAKENED

After 4.19. Revolution the second republic appeared (1960 – 1961). Yoon Bo-Sun was the president and it was the parliamentary [cabinet] government system. So, Chang Myun, the Premier, actually had the power of government. He tried to establish and keep order socially and politically, but the different opinions between statesmen caused ceaseless demonstrations on the streets.

Chang Myun's government could not properly cope with the struggle of the statesmen and the various demonstrations.

This disorder caused 5.16. Coup d'e-tat.

On May 16, 1962 General Park, Chung Hee's regime began.

He took the power by coup d'e-tat (but he called it revolution).

He was born in a poor farmer's family and became a president of Korea. He was a teacher of an elementary school under the rule of Japanese imperialism. He quitted teaching in three years and entered the Japanese military academy in Manchuria to become an officer. After the liberation from Japan he became an officer of South Korean army. He began to confer about the coup in 1952 and he made a coup successfully on May 16, 1962.

He had a zeal for economic development. He with zeal focused on exporting from 1964. He pushed full-scaled drive of export taking the lead of the Committee of Export Promotion and achieved US$10,000,000,000 of export in 1977. He achieved the Korean economy's high level growth, called, "The Miracle of the Han River".

He had the Seoul-Busan Expressway constructed and Po-Hang Steel Company established as well, which enabled to make autos and ship as well as all kinds of constructions. He set up and prepared the basic production factors and the infrastructure.

Now, Korea holds the first in rank in IT industries, in ship building industries in the world. Economically it holds world-widely the 10th -12th in rank by assessment of GDP. It holds the 8th in rank by assessment of exporting in the world.

Korea was a country which received the financial aid, but now it became a country giving financial aid.

To the surprise it is marked as the 2nd place after America in dispatching Christian missionaries world-widely.

The coup d'e-tat always is supposed to bring bloodshed.

However the 5.16 coup d'e-tat did not bring any bloodshed.

What is meant by that?

It means the majority of Korean people did not go against it.

Therefore we can call it the successful "Bloodless Revolution".

TURBULENT TIMES

I and those of my generation were attending school during the turbulent times. We had been through World War Two and Korean War. We studied in a tent or a temporary school structure. I was attending school by train from Kim-Hae to Busan. I had to study in the cabin of the train because the train never ran by schedule.

Two or three hour delay was common. Sometimes four hour delay occurred. It caused me to try to get on the free-truck-ride to get to school in time.

In the train there were a few seats in a cabin and most of the cabins did not have lights. I had to try to occupy a seat on the floor under the light to study. Most of time was spent to memorize the new words of English and in memorizing idioms and the grammar.

I could not spend much time for the other subjects.

I recollect and regret I did not do my best.

It was not my effort but it was the result of the gift given from birth come from above.

Our generation did not have education in the good situation.

We could not eat well. We did not have good clothes. We went through Korean War and 4.19 Revolution that we fought against the dictatorial and corrupt government of Rhee Syngman. We as students had to run out to the street for demonstration very often.

I am afraid we did not learn as much as we should. However, we learned how to respect our parents and the seniors. We learned how to love brothers and sisters. We learned how to love neighbors. We loved our country Korea even though it did not give us a thing because it was so poor. I believe our patriotism and our hard work made Korea as the boastful country. South Korea did not have any natural resources but man power. Our generation just worked hard.

The younger generation which did not go through the difficulties of the 1950-53 Korean War cannot understand the tragedy caused by the communists' cruelty. During the lost ten years (1998-2007) of Kim, Dae Joong and Ro, Moo Hyun's leftwing regime they misled the young under the pretext of progressivism. They taught and misguided to abuse the old simply as conservative; the old who have fulfilled the present economic development of Korea.

I am afraid that the asinine activity of the young generation inevitably resulted from the lack of the understanding about the North Korea's communism. You, young generation, may say that the role is different according to the time and season, but you cannot play the decisive role if you do not know the time and season correctly. As I experienced the communists' tyranny I cannot help trembling at the thought of what kind of tragedy would be brought to Korea by the lost ten years (1998-2007).

I do think Kim, Dae Joong and Ro, Moo Hyun are dangerous men.

ATTENDING CHRISTIAN SCHOOL

It was a great fortune that I came to attend a Christian school. Dae Kwang (Great Light) Junior and High school was established by Dr. & Rev. Han, Kyung-Jik who won the Templeton Prize in 2003, who was the senior pastor of Young-Nak Presbyterian Church in Seoul. At that time it was the biggest church in the world. Most of students who were attending the school were from northern Korea and grown up in Christian families. We had worship service in the morning before classes and also after classes. The teachers were Christians. We had bible study. We also had an hour of English bible study in a week through an American missionary. We learned to be dutiful to our parents, patriotism and Christian love.

I would say my personality was formed in this Christian school.

I was good academically in the school.

I was loved by good teachers.

I started to attend the dawn prayer meeting from the ninth grade.

Until tenth grade I wanted to be a law man but around the end of the tenth grade I changed my mind to become a medical doctor.

I became to believe that the life helping other people was the precious one. I came to believe the doctor is the best one to live a life helping other people. I firmly determined to be a doctor.

I entered the medical school of Yon-sei University, formerly

Severance Medical School which had been established by Dr. N.H.

Allen (came to Korea in 1884), an American missionary --- The founder of Severance Hospital (Yon-seiUniversity medical school) and Horace Underwood (1885), an American missionary --- The founder of Yon-sei University, of Korea Bible Society, of SaeMoonAn Presbyterian Church. I finished premedical course and one semester of main course. I was obliged to change my course because of our financial situation which grew from bad to worse after my father's critical surgery of stomach.

TURNING POINT

It has been already one week since I began to visit this tomb place carrying the heavy Gray's Anatomy under my arm after school.

The Severance Hospital and the medical school were located at the western end of Mount Namsan facing the Seoul rail road station and our home was at the end of the other side of the mountain.

Along the ridge of Mount Namsan I could come home.

The tomb was situated a little off from the road.

It was a very quiet spot.

The place was not the graveyard.

Just a single grave alone was there lonely at the mountainside of Mount Namsan located in the center of Seoul City.

The grave was anything but a pile of soil covered with turfs and weeds.

It did not have any tombstone.

I guessed it might have been one of the dead during the Korean War.

Gloomily, I was reflecting my junior high period.

I could have seen so many bodies deserted in the gorges during the Korean War. What a dreadful tragedy it was!

With my own eyes I saw over 10 bodies with their hands tied behind had been shot to death by communists.

The communists were not in military uniform, but in plain clothes. I have seen the cruel brutality of the communists.

In an instant I was also reflecting of my elementary school period before the Korean War jumping around and up and down this Namsan mountainside with friends.

I would climb up the cherry trees to pick a handful of cherries.

I would enjoy the fresh juice of the cherries.

I was smiling without my awareness thinking of my friends' faces smudged by cherry juices in purple color.

The tomb was at the breast of the mountain.

I thought this dead was rather lucky comparing with many others because this at least was shrouded with soil and weeds to hide his (her) body. The grave was shaped like a breast.

I sentimentally lay down with my back against the grave. Naturally and simultaneously the whole sky came into my eyes.

The cloud was flowing smoothly.

I felt so close to the one who was laid in the tomb.

I had a dream as a doctor, but my dream was going to fade away.

I thought of suicide.

I thought I could understand why one killed oneself.

However, I was compelled to make a certain decision to quit studying medicine or something clear.

My father was operating a small cotton mill with ten or twelve weaving looms, but he had to leave the mill to his friend since he had had a difficult surgery of gastric ulcer which made him stay away from work over one year. I did not understand the exact reason why the plant was not good enough to support our family after less than one year since my father's surgery. Anyhow, since my father's surgery our family's financial situation grew from bad to worse quickly.

Two years past since his surgery. I had to have a part time job till 11:00 pm after school to support myself and partially my family. My mother opened a little mama and papa grocery store to earn a living.

I could hardly have time to study.

I could not bear the bad result of the academic record, which made me visit this place almost for a week.

I thought I had to decide something, but I could not think of any refreshing and sharp pointed way.

I got up and left the place taking my way toward the English Institute, my work place where I was teaching English grammar.

Evening was falling fast.

In the bus I came to decide to rest from school.

Right away I thought of my mother, who was bearing all hardship because of me. How happy she was when I entered the medial school which was one of the best in medicine in Korea!

It was my first concern how I could comfort my mother.

I loved my mother very much. She gave me birth to me after her bone breaking pain. Since I happened to see her giving birth to my youngest sister Haesun (Sunny) I became to love and respect her much further more.

How much she would be disappointed!

How guilty she would feel due to her helpless situation!

I still remember her weeping at night under her blanket to avoid my awareness.

As I got to the English Institute I became busy in teaching.

Another week later, I visited Professor Lee, Jung Hwan, Dean of Business and Economy College. He gave me the permission to transfer to the business administration course from medical course.

I was eager in my study until my junior high with a desire to become a lawyer in the future.

As my faith in God was growing mature I came to be interested in helping others, which made me work with the object of being a medical doctor.

Eventually it made me enter the medical school.

My purpose of life became simple.

It was to serve neighbors instead of pursuing my fame and fortune. The very day, Friday, June 3, 1959, was the turning point of my life.

Two days before I visited Professor Lee I was coming home from the school after I visited the tomb place.

I looked down my neighborhood and came to see a little school building in the midst of pine trees --- The school where I would run around freely with my friends.

As I see the school building it seemed as a beautiful hospital building in a flash. That's it. 'Now I cannot become a doctor to fulfill my dream, but I can become a businessman and if God allows me material blessings to buy that building I will run the hospital to fulfill my dream.

As a hospital owner I was going to visit each one of patients and offer a bible and introduce Jesus Christ to them. If I find out some patients who are unable to pay the medical bill I was going to let them go home for free of charge quietly. This was my simple dream.

As a natural consequence I was transferred to the business administration course from the medical course and I finished the business administration course with B. A. degree in 1963.

BROAD-MINDED PEOPLE

I knocked at the door of the dean of the medical college.

Dr. Kim, Myung Sun welcomed me with a smiling face.

I explained the reason why I had to transfer to the business administration course.

He listened to me explaining my situation and he said,

"Yes, there would be too many doctors in the future and the doctors might solicit to cure patients from alley to alley shouting

'Cure disease'. You made the right decision. You'd better be an entrepreneur to give a lot of jobs to the people."

He was the man who had broad outlook of life. He had an insight into things. He knew how to encourage people. He knew I had nothing but the very choice.

When I paid a visit to the house of Professor Lee, Dean of Business and Economy College he was not in. His wife asked me the reason why I want to see him. After she heard my story she asked me to wait for him. The dinner time was drawing near and

I was going to leave the place. Mrs. Lee told me to wait a little longer and eat dinner with them. Her earnest favor was so strong that I could not refuse it. As soon as Professor Lee came home meal was served.

He said, *"I am not a Christian but I want to pray to thank for the food."*

I asked him. *"You just said you are not a Christian but you want to pray. Why?"*

He said, *"Because I feel I can have daily bread not only by my effort but also by dint of someone else."*

I explained the reason of my visiting him.

He said, *" Yon-Sei medical school is the most difficult one to enter in this country. I feel so sorry for you in such a situation. However, if you want to transfer to the Business Administration course I will gladly accept your transfer."*

I thus graduated in Business Administration from Yon-Sei University instead of medicine in 1963.

ONE-DAY HONEYMOON

Dear my children,

Your mom and I got married on Saturday, October 23, 1965 at Shin IL Presbyterian Church at Yaksoo-dong, Sungdong-Gu(now Joong-Gu), Seoul, Korea, which had been established by Rev. Rhee, Il Sun in 1947.

It was my mother church where I was grown up in Christ from Sunday school all through to be a deacon. Rev. Rhee was a zealous pastor in many ways. He was also a doctor of medicine.

He established this church beating a drum and walking around the village of Yaksoo-dong.

At that time your mom was teaching in the attached elementary school of Ehwa Womans University and I was working for the Universal Travel Service – at that time it was an airline agent as an IATA member. My job was to take care of the travelers who were traveling to foreign countries. In 1960s Korea was a very poor country. However, most of the travelers were people of wealth. Naturally the airline service was a fancy job at that time in Korea. The office was much fancier than the other business offices.

We got married on Saturday afternoon and spent one night at Walker Hill Hotel at Kwangnaru, in the suburban area of Seoul City.

On Monday we went to work. We were happy though because we had workplace. At that time so many college graduates could not have workplace.

A HYBRID AT HOME

As I mentioned before your mom was teaching the second grade in the elementary school attached to Ewha Womans University in Seoul. The elementary school was one of the excellent private schools whose students were from the rich and the most educated.

It was a warm and balmy spring day in 1966.

When I came home from work a hybrid little girl with golden hair was waiting for me. My wife told me that she had brought her from an orphanage. I would rather say that she was a special product of the Korean War to avoid the sympathetic feeling. Her father was an unknown American GI and her mother was a Korean woman.

Your mom said, *"Her adoption procedure to an American family is on process. As soon as the adoption procedure is finished she is supposed to go to America."*

Mom also explained that she was entrusted to our family until the adoption procedure gets done. The purpose of entrusting her to our family was to give her proper family education to break off the bad habits that she had obtained from the orphanage.

She had about ten bad habits at that time. It was not surprising that most of her bad habits were related with food. Providing food was limited in the orphanage. Limited food caused her to get bad habits; eating in haste, crying for food, uneasiness, lack of stability, studying our faces and etc.

By way of illustration I bought a few boxes of cookies for her on the way home from work and gave her one box out of three and put the other ones on the shelf. Even if I assured her that the other ones on the shelf were all hers and she could have them later she felt uneasy to cry for them until I gave her all of them. As soon as she got them she ate them in haste until she ate all of them. She stayed with us for one year and a half. We did not have any idea why the adoption procedure took so long. At any rate we could not break off all of her bad habits.

Unexpectedly her adoption procedure took over one year and six months.

When she left Korea for America I wrote a letter to the foster parents about her bad habits and also a few of simple Korean words like pee and feces for urgent time. I put it into her pocket.

시 Poem

당신이 보고싶어!
왜 가슴이 아플 때
당신의 말씀을 읽어야
그 뜻이 보입니까?

왜 마음이 슬플 때
당신의 말씀을 읽어야
가슴에 다가옵니까?

왜 눈물이 가득한 어른 거리는
눈으로 당신의 말씀을 보아야
찰나(刹那)가 아닌 영원(永遠)이 보입니까?

주님
꼭
아픔이어야 합니까?
슬픔이어야 합니까?
눈물이어야 합니까?

당신이 보고싶어
아픔을 인내(忍耐)합니다
슬픔을 달랩니다
눈물을 삼킵니다

1971년 5월 이영근 씀

Longing to see you!
Why am I able to perceive the meaning of Your Word
as I read it with my heart in pain?

Why does Your Word touch my soul
as I read it with my heart in grief?

Why am I able to see not the instant but
the eternity as I read Your Word with my
blurry eyes filled with tears?

Lord,
by all means
Should it be pain?
Should it be sorrow?
Should it be tears?

Longing to see You,
I endure pain.
I appease sorrow.
I swallow tears.

composed by Young G. Lee in May 1971

DAD, WHAT MADE YOU COME TO AMERICA?*

"Dad, what made you come to America?"

Helen asked me. To this question I would say as follows:

I came to this country not for better life of faith like the Puritan (Pilgrim) Fathers, not for better education for my children and not for better eating, clothing and dwelling. I was satisfied with our church life in Korea. We had freedom of faith. Mom and I had good income to have a decent house which was fully paid. Deliberately saying the main reason was the difficulties which came from the dealings with the corruptible execution of civil officials in 1960's in Korea.

The government employees wanted "under-table money" for every case. Even though all the required documents were prepared properly and met their requirements the officials did not proceed to settle the case. They stalled for time and held the documents in their drawers to induce offering bribes. The compromising with the civil officials had to be continued whether I like it or not.

I loathed it more than a snake. I could not stand compromising with the officials. Bribery was rampant everywhere among the officials.

I felt no hope to escape from that situation as long as I earn a living in Korea because even private business could not stay away from the government employees. I decided first to leave Korea. Studying abroad was the only way to escape from the situation at that time. I took the examination studying abroad. The examination was controlled by the Ministry of Education Affairs and I had to pass two subjects: Korean history and English. As soon as I passed the examination I mailed out letters with the TOFEL TEST result to ten universities in America. The first response was from Oregon State University with the I-20 Form.

It was so difficult for ordinary people to get entering visa to America at that time, but there was no problem for the regular students who had passed the examination studying abroad controlled by the Ministry of Education Affairs. Korea was so poor that it allowed only US$50.00 to the regular student for the travel fund and $30.00 to the other travelers at that time.

I left Korea in 1968.

"This is the right country."

I began to attend the first term of the Oregon State University at Corvallis, Oregon in spring 1969. My major was MBA.

I was invited to a private family by the school program for the freshmen. They had two children. The host was a mailman.

He and his wife were so kind and observed the proprieties to me.

They showed me all the pictures which had been taken during their trip in European countries. I had a good meal and good time.

I was impressed by their peaceful living in comfort.

It was a dream-like story at that time in Korea that a mailman could have a travel to Europe.

A mailman could barely make a living at that time notwithstanding the hard work in Korea.

I wrote a letter to my wife about my experience of the visit to the family;

"Korea is left behind one hundred years (?) than the States."

Buddhism and Confucianism contributed to the aristocrats and the royal authority. Both religions enjoyed with those who had power and wealth. They did not contribute anything to the powerless and the poor. They just taught them to live "like water and like wind".

They taught them "Persons of low birth live lowly."

They did not break down the barrier of classes.

They did nothing about human rights for years of thousands.

They just said "karma"- retribution for the deeds of former life.

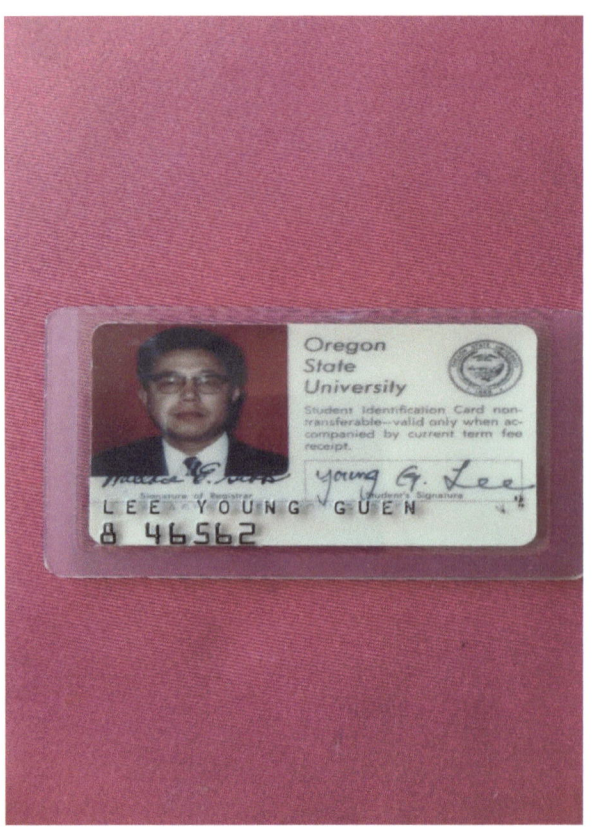

In 1972, I was once operating a sandwich shop. One day I received a letter to appear at the civil office indicating that I did not provide the workman's compensation insurance. I did not know it was mandatory for an employer to provide workman's compensation insurance to the employees. I insured through an agent and visited the office to show the insurance policy. I handed out the policy to the civil clerk with the relevant letter from the office. The clerk said, *"This is what I need."* smiling at me and made a copy for her file. I smiled back and said *"Thank you."* to the clerk. Coming out of the office I said to myself: *"This is the right country for me to live in."* If I had been in such a case in Korea I should have called a few friends to find out if there were any ones who had relationship with the civil officer to resolve this problem.

I should have assumed a low posture as if I were a criminal in front of the clerk. I would not want to imagine the Korean civil clerk's attitude.

Woe is Korea! At that time we did not have even such a system. "Workmen's compensation insurance" – They couldn't even dream of such a thing.

Thereafter, I never had any occurrence to see any civil clerks or government employees. All I had to do was to pay tax to Uncle Sam properly.

I can feel the governance of the U.S. government when I pay tax only. In Korea the governance always existed in our main living room at that time. I do not know about it of today in Korea and hope the status is better. I hear civil clerks' service has been changed much better.

Then, what are the high rank government officers' embezzlements of huge amount of money?

시 Poem

아담이 미웠다.
나는 아담이 미웠다.
에덴동산에 있는 모든 것을 다 가지고 있으면서도
그 중 단 하나를 하나님께 양보하지 않은
아담이 미웠다.

나는 내가 미웠다.
아담을 닮은 내가 미웠다.
열을 가지고 있으면서도
하나를 구별하기를 싫어하는 내가 미웠다.

나는 늘 그랬고 지금도 그렇다.
하나를 사랑하지 못하면서
아홉에게서 사랑을 받기를 원하는 내가 밉다

나는 내가 죄인인 것을 알게 되었다.
아담이 미웠었는데 불쌍히 여기게 되었다.
하나가 아까웠었는데
열이 다 주의 것임을 알게 되었다.

나는 내가 빛의 자식임을 알았다.
빛이요 소금임을 알았다. Salt as well.
나는 내가 죽어도 산다는 것을 알았다.
더 좋은 부활을 얻고자 죽음을 택하는 뜻을 알았다.

나는 복음을 자랑하게 되었다.
나에게 남은 날이 있어 늦지 않았다는 것을 알았다.
불쌍한 아담을 찾아 간다.
하나를 사랑하려고 두 손을 벌려 본다.

I Hated Adam.
I hated Adam 'cause he did not
yield just one single thing to God
though he had everything in Eden.
I did hate him.

I hated myself.
Me having taken after Adam
'cause I had ten, but unwilling
to set one aside for the tithes.

I used to be always so and now is also same.
Not loving even one, I hate myself expecting
to be loved by nine others.

I came to know I am a sinner.
I hated Adam, but now feel sorry for him.
Having been stingy with one, but now
I reckon ten all belong to the Lord.

I came to realize I am a son of the Light,
I came to realize I shall live
In Him even though I die.
I came to know why some rather
choose death for "better resurrection".
I came to be proud of the Gospel.
I knew it was not too late
'cause my days are remained.
I go for the pathetic Adams.
I open my arms to love one.

On October 7, 1986 Composed by Young G. Lee

Do you have a job opening?

I was told to visit the places where jobs seemed available in Los Angeles downtown. I went in an office parlor of a certain company and there were a young man and a young woman filling out the applications. The lady clerk said to those two persons handing in their applications,

"We will let you know when the job is available."

I talked to myself that they did not have a job opening at the present time. I should be hurry to finish filling out this application and go to another place. At that time I could see a gentleman approaching to the clerk and say something. I handed in the application and the clerk said to me to come in. She led me to the gentleman's office. He examined my application and asked me when I could start to work. I said, *"From tomorrow"*

In that afternoon I started to look for an apartment for rent.

MEETING MR. TOCHSTAD

It was quite natural for me to start to look for a work to earn a living and earn tuition as soon as I got to Los Angeles before starting to study. As you can guess I did not have enough living expenses in the first place. That was why I had to find a job.

In 1968 the immigration law was not so strict but rather generous that I could work without any work-permit. The Social Security number was issued easily right away upon applying it.

I was looking for a dwelling place. I saw a sign for RENT in a front lawn yard of the house at 1312 Write St. Los Angeles, where now the Los Angeles Convention Center is located. I was standing there and looking at the sign. An old man was approaching to me. He introduced himself as the owner of the house. He asked me if I was a married person. I said, *" Yes I am a married man but my wife and children are in Korea and I am here by myself for further study."* He said, *"If you are a single now I cannot rent it to you."* He added, *"I rented it to a single boy and had enough troubles and I am looking for a Christian couple."* I said, *"I am a Christian."*

He said, *"You are a Christian and then let's go inside and talk."*

We shared a little conversation in the living room and he held me by my two hands to pray with him.

He prayed, *"Lord, thank you for bringing Mr. Lee to me and …."*

I prayed after him, *"Thank you, Lord, for guiding me to meet Mr. Tochstad and….."* He rented me a room by his living room. I was told to share the living room and the kitchen with him. I told him about the smell of Kimchi. He smiled at me saying *"It is Okay. I also eat stench cheese."*

He was an immigrant from Sweden. He said he used to have had two jobs when young. He was living alone. He said, *"When I was young I could not meet girls because I did not have money. Now I have money but I cannot meet girls because I am old."* He was a good Christian.

AMERICAN DREAM

"American dream"; this terms is usually used when someone made a great accomplishment in business or made a good success in obtaining a great fame. Nevertheless, my American dream was to live free from illegality and corruption.

I think the terms, "American dream" should be used not only in attaining great materials or a great fame but also in attaining spiritual satisfaction and remaining in Him like the Puritan (Pilgrim) Fathers' wish.

Dear children, do not live on Good Friday, but on Easter.

Closing my story until I entered this country I want to say again that I have been blessed by my God. The decisive evidence is that all my children know our father God and serve him as their God.

Here I want to introduce one shocking bible verse: *"After that whole generation had been gathered to their fathers, another generation grew up, who knew neither the Lord nor what He had done for Israel."(Judges 2:10-11)*

EPILOGUE

Success and fail both exist in the non-Christian life, but there is success only in the Christian life of faith.

First, we should define what success of life is.

Is it to make a lot of money and live in a big house driving Mercedes-Benz?

No. Definitely it is not.

Our success of life is to live well in God's will and providence.

I once had a great opportunity to make a lot of money. I do say a lot of money. However, the business was stopped by God. I would dare say "by God". He showed me that I could make a lot of money if He wants to allow me. He just let me taste it. I once succeeded in my undertaking and also failed, but I was successful in my spiritual life because my faith in Christ became much more abundant. I would often look back on my past assuming that I became a medical doctor without any hindrance. I could become a very proud man because I might not experience any difficulties and afflictions. Hallelujah! He made me as a businessman which did not fit to me and made me experience a lot of difficulties, afflictions, being humiliated and disgrace as well as plenty.

"Not only so, but we also rejoice in our sufferings, because we know that suffering produces perseverance; perseverance. character; and character, hope." Romans (5:3-4)

If the Lord allows me I would like to write a long story of mine in the title of "Beyond the Jordan".

I want to say three things to you closing my story up to the top of Mount Pisgah from Ur of the Chaldeans.

Firstly,

Please **teach your children His words** and how faithful the Lord has been to our family so that your children may not go astray.

Secondly,

Let your children **have the certain two identities:**

1. **You are Korean-Americans for James and Helen's children.**
2. **You are God's children.**

   This latter identity is the most important one for you.

   Always remember how Jesus was tempted by the devil;

   (1) "**If you are the Son of God**, tell these stones to become bread."

   (2) "**If you are the Son of God**, throw yourself down."

Do remember how the devil uses the identity.
***Devil always tempts you with your identity.
Do not forget you are God's children.

Thirdly,

Have a dream in God's providence. It is the way for Christians to dream that I did not know when young. Joseph did not dream to be a ruler of Egypt when young and even did not understand what his dreams meant because they were not Joseph's dreams but God's.

Joseph came to understand his dreams after he became the second ruler of Egypt.
Joseph just sought His kingdom first and His righteousness.

I have been living in America for 51 years.
I would say I love America because it has allowed me to get what I needed physically and spiritually.
I shall see my children will live on this land worshipping the Lord.
I will pray for my children on the top of Mount Pisgah as Moses did. This is *the land flowing with milk and honey.*

I will not be lazy to pray for my children, Korea, Mexico and America this land.
America in my prayer cannot become Egypt.

God bless America, land that I know.
Stand beside her and guide her.
Through the night with a light from above.
From the mountain to the prairie,
To the ocean with white foam.
God bless America, my home sweet home.
God bless America, my home sweet home.

CPSIA information can be obtained
at www.ICGtesting.com
Printed in the USA
BVHW020832170619
551188BV00005B/40/P